Our Witness

Blessings
Dwight Hart

OUR WITNESS

THE BATTLE TO LIVE THROUGH A RARE AND INCAPACITATING DISEASE

by Timesia M. Hart
with Genet Jones

XULON PRESS

Xulon Press
2301 Lucien Way #415
Maitland, FL 32751
407.339.4217
www.xulonpress.com

Unless otherwise indicated, Scripture quotations taken from the King
James Version (KJV) – *public domain.*

Glossary definitions reprinted with permission from:

Guthy Jackson Foundation
8910 University Center Lane, Suite 725
San Diego, CA 92122
Phone: (858) 638-7638
info@guthyjacksonfoundation.org
www.guthyjacksonfoundation.org

Printed in the United States of America

Paperback ISBN-13: 978-1-5456-8038-4
Ebook ISBN-13: 978-1-5456-8039-1

To my parents,
John & Ethel Minniefield Sr.

In Loving Memory:

John H. Minniefield Sr.

Doris Marie Hebert

Joanne Williams (Granny)

William (Uncle Bo) Carter

Blanche Carter (Aunt Blanche)

Pastor Arthur Trainer

Glen Brown

Joy Sanders

King Mar

Michael W. Callihan

Pat Payne

Coach Ken Boken

Janet Pate

Xander Moore

Dr. and Mrs. Leigh

Rodney Roberson

Freddie Joe Hawkins

Rhoda
Onyebueke (Ma Ma)

CONTENTS

FOREWORD

I love Timesia Hart. She has spunk. You know, the kind of spunk that is sassy yet sweet, funny yet kind. We have laughed so hard at times I think I'm going to just die, and cried so hard I couldn't see. Timesia's love of God literally "oozes" out of her. She has an abiding faith in God that transcends the abilities of man, as her testimony gives witness.

By definition, a warrior is a brave or experienced soldier or fighter. A lion is a symbol of strength and courage, and a lioness is independent, fierce, and brave.

Timesia Hart embodies the strength and courage of a lion—as you will quickly discover with each turn of the page as you follow her fight against the unknown. *Our Witness* is a compelling, heart-driven memoir of an independent, brave, and fiercely determined lioness clawing herself free from a world of unknowns, and you will be at the edge of your seat and bewildered about how she succeeded.

But if there were a word to describe Timesia Hart—it must be *warrior*! Timesia Hart is a brave and experienced soldier and she is, against all odds, the quintessential fighter. Your definition of warrior will change once you read *Our Witness*.

God sustained Timesia, guided her, protected her, and healed her through the journey of discovery, treatment, and healing of the rare neurological disease neuromyelitis optica (NMO). I am so thankful Timesia is sharing her story with you. A warrior knows nothing is ever wasted, especially a story shared with such humility and transparency. I pray these pages bring you much hope!

—Susan Goss, December 2019

INTRODUCTION

T his is not a happy ending story.

If you are looking for ten steps on how to cope with a rare disease, or three tips on how to live after the doctor has told you to prepare to die, this isn't that book. I'm past the point of trying to impress anyone with another unbelievable story, in which I pretend to have all the answers that will magically apply to your situation and make everything perfect.

Instead, this book is my attempt to offer a resting place where you can stop for a moment and know that you aren't the only one who has traveled this way. It is my prayer that somewhere down the road, if you encounter a life-altering trial, you will have tucked away a couple of nuggets from this book that help you take the next step.

When I read self-help books, I find it difficult to connect unless I've experienced the problem myself. This is why *Our Witness* shares my story through many eyes: those of a loving spouse, a parent, children, siblings, and of course myself, the patient. You are almost certain to fit one of those categories, and I hope the perspective will help connect our journey to your own.

To anyone who is suffering or has a loved one suffering from a disease: this book is to offer you hope and encouragement. It is my intention to be transparent; therefore, some parts of the book may be difficult to read. I believe that being honest about how we arrived on this side of our trials is pertinent for your journey. I want you to be encouraged to keep putting one foot in front of the other. This journey hasn't been easy, but remaining intentionally hopeful has strengthened us throughout.

It has been said that everyone falls into one of three categories: in a trial, coming out of a trial, or headed into a trial. This is why *Our Witness* is relevant for anyone. I will lead you through my experience with a scary, debilitating, and rare disease, doing my best to provide encouragement to support you in your own trials.

I want to spread awareness about my disease, neuromyelitis optica, and share how I am embracing a new normal, including finding my own healing through outreach for others. I also hope and pray that anyone reading this book who lacks hope or doesn't believe in miracles will have a new understanding of the power of Jesus Christ.

Much of how we survived this disease was by encouraging ourselves with the word of God. The Holy Bible remains a vital entity in our journey moving forward, and I have included many of my favorite Bible verses at the end of the book.

Like I said, mine is not a happy ending story—yet. But I am keeping that door open to see what God does with the rest of my life.

MY LIFE BEFORE NMO

I was born in our home on my mother's birthday, with only the midwife and my grandmother present. My father was working at a service station, back in the day when you received service: the attendant pumped your gas, wiped your windshield, and checked your tires. One of the travelers who came through that day was named Timesia, so my father picked that name for me.

I was born dark-skinned, and was referred to as the "chubby black girl" most of my life. Mother was a great cook, and I liked to eat. It seemed like I ate the same amount as my sisters and brothers, but they never gained weight like I did. I learned later that I had an autoimmune condition called hypothyroidism, which shed some light on why my weight was a problem. I eventually had a complete "thyroid storm," and am now on medication for the rest of my life.

I had a pretty normal life as the fifth from the oldest in a blended family of ten. My mother says that I was also the one (there is at least one in every family) who stayed in trouble. Mother says she and Daddy knew I would require an enormous amount of extra discipline when, after telling me many times to stay off the heater, they had to peel me from it with second- and third-degree burns on the insides of my legs and upper arms.

My teenage years were typical, except for having the strictest Daddy ever. Daddy was very smart, even though he had only completed the third grade due to having to work on the farm. I never understood how he knew that if anything went wrong, I was the culprit; but he did. He had a way of dealing with the situation that still impacts my life today. The entire time I was down, I knew my Daddy was praying for me. Some of the most authentic prayers in the world, over any matter in our family, were those my Daddy prayed. Mother knew that, and would call when I was in the hospital, asking Daddy to pray for me.

Our neighborhood, Lakeside Park, was very safe. We were allowed to go to school, church, and anywhere in our neighborhood, as long as we were back home by the time the street lights came on. We rode our bikes, played street softball and kickball, talked, and had many jacks and jump-rope competitions. In my neighborhood the older girls mentored the younger girls. They were a part of Camp Fire Girls (like the Girl Scouts), so when I was a little Blue Bird, they were the babysitters, learning how to wash clothes, prepare meals, and sew, in addition to making good grades in school. Both of my parents worked, which was true for most households by then. The older girls in the community had to step up, and I looked forward to being the older girl to serve as a mentor for the younger girls coming behind me.

I did get to become a Camp Fire Girl, participate in 4H clubs, and become the mentor I'd longed to be. I didn't do well with sewing, though. I was too impatient, and wanted to be able to start an outfit at four o'clock and have it ready to wear by seven.

The last two years of high school, I had the opportunity to go to a technical school to become a licensed cosmetologist. It was such an accomplishment to graduate high school with a cosmetology license. I worked for one year in a barbershop, for an owner who allowed me to be part of the process of remodeling his shop.

After saving some money, I decided to go on to college. I'd always wanted to continue my education, but I knew my parents couldn't afford it. In the fall the year after graduating high school, I enrolled at Huston-Tillotson University in Austin, Texas, 250 miles from home. It was very difficult to focus when I was concerned about how I would get through the school year financially. I worked a part-time job during the semester and learned first-hand how expensive an education was, which made me very grateful to be in school. I had applied for a work-study program for the following semester, and that made it easier to enjoy the holiday break.

Over Christmas break, 1981, I just needed to spend quality time with my family. I intended to come up with a better long-term plan as soon as I was back in Austin.

3

But when I visited my good friend at home in Port Arthur, Texas, she told me about an amazing chance for us to travel the world and serve our country at the same time. She said she had been looking into the program in order to travel, and she had been told that there was a deal called the "buddy system," which allowed both you and your bestie to join the program together, go through the training together, and maybe even be stationed in the same unit, like a permanent party.

I didn't realize that the great program she was talking about was the United States Army, and when I found out, I told her that I didn't know anything about the Army. She assured me that was the reason you go in with a buddy.

Let me tell you about my buddy system: it broke down right at the very beginning, at the in-processing center. At this point you've taken your placement testing and have selected your military career, and you go to the processing center for a final quick medical exam. You are then rushed on to be sworn in, hustled onto an aircraft, and away you go. I noticed that my buddy was going one way and I was being hurried in the opposite direction. I kept trying to tell the sergeants in charge that I was on the "buddy system" and my buddy wasn't with me. One sergeant in the entire building finally gave me some hope and said that he would go find out what was going on, but in the meantime, I needed to go ahead with the in-processing procedures.

I never saw that sergeant again, and my behind went on without a buddy to Fort Jackson, South Carolina, for Basic

Training, and Fort McLennan, Alabama, for Advanced Individual Training. The next time I saw my friend with the great idea to join the Army on the "buddy system" was on Thanksgiving leave, when she told me that a medical issue kept her from passing her physical.

Within a few days of being on active duty, I knew enough about the Army to decide I would just like to get back home. Fortunately, the Army doesn't just let you go back home because you want to. Looking back, that was the most structured time in my adult life. No wardrobe issues, no worries about dinner, no need to plan my day. Thanks to my parents, the respect part of the military was a no-brainer. I was familiar with listening to and following orders, after all the extra discipline I received growing up.

My leadership skills landed me a squad leader position the third week of Basic Training. That's one job I could have done without; nevertheless, I was given an order, and it had to be carried out. That position forced me to assume responsibility for my entire squad of ten, including myself. I had to learn a lot in a short amount of time, and have been better for it ever since.

The most challenging part of Basic Training was qualifying with my weapon. I'd never fired a weapon, and after our block of instruction in which engaging the enemy took on a stronger meaning for me, I was afraid. My drill sergeant came to my post, dropped to a prone position beside me, and explained that if I didn't fire at the enemy, he would take the shot at me, then move on to my team.

I decided that was not an option. It took me two tries to qualify with my M16, but I did, and later became the M60 machine gunner for my company (and the M60 was a much larger weapon than the M16). I'd enlisted to be in the Military Police, but later had to get real and become a Personnel Records Specialist (a distinguished name for a secretary), a more realistic fit for my skill set.

I overcame being away from home pretty quickly. In the military, you realize that everybody is away from home, so your platoon learns to function as a family. In some ways, I grew up in the military. It is certainly where my adult life started.

On the bus back to Fort Hood, Texas, after being home on leave, I met a man who was also from Port Arthur. We were from the same small town, yet our paths had never crossed until we were both in the Army, both headed back to our posts early from being on leave. Coincidence? I didn't think so. He didn't think too much about it, but I thought, *This doesn't make sense unless we are supposed to be together.*

He had recently been moved from San Antonio to be permanently stationed at Fort Hood. His company was eight blocks from mine. He was a diehard Dallas Cowboys fan, and so was I. He asked for my unit info, I gave it to him, and we went our separate ways. It wasn't long before we were talking regularly, and things quickly progressed. This man was very kind, considerate, charming, and a star football player in his unit, and I never doubted his love for me.

Michael and I were married in the post chapel, and planned to save money to take a trip later. Two years later our family expanded with the birth of our first daughter, Naeaidria. Michael finished his military service and went to work for the government at the post gymnasium, while I re-enlisted for four more years, and shortly afterward received orders for Germany. I moved to Mannheim, Germany, after packing up for the movers, while Michael worked on his and Naeaidria's passports. After two months, I was able to get quarters (family housing) for us, and Michael and Nae joined me.

Our next orders were to Fort Drum, New York (also known as Snow Country, USA), in October, 1991. Watertown, NY, was the nearest city with a hospital, so that was where Tyresia was born. New York was far from home, but we were thankful that she was born stateside and not in Germany.

We decided that I would not re-enlist, and that we would move back to Port Arthur after being away for so long.

Two years after going back home, our marriage was in ruins due to Michael's struggles with addiction. For the first time in my life, I had an encounter with hopelessness. I just didn't know what to do. We were like any other married couple — we had our ups and downs — but we had always managed to resolve our issues.

Michael was a good husband and father. Separating was the last thing on my mind. I clearly remember one night in such despair that I placed my knees on either side of my

Bible and cried out to God, telling Him I couldn't make another move before hearing from Him. I loved Michael, and he was a good man who had simply lost his way. The vows we took were so important for me to keep, and I intended to fight for the future of our family. I didn't want myself or my two girls to become statistics.

I remember thanking God in advance for restoring our marriage. I wanted to come through this raging storm still happily married, in order to encourage other couples that nothing is impossible with God. I have always thought the way to be an effective witness is by experience. I knew God was faithful even though I hadn't experienced anything like what we were facing.

I made excuses for Michael for a long time. I wanted to save my marriage, but this battle couldn't be won with me fighting and him not.

I didn't know how to confront him, so I called over his mother and my parents. After we told him we all wanted him to go get some help, Michael made his decision, packed a gym bag, told me not to blame myself, and walked out the front door. He said he was sorry, but he didn't need any help. I was left to deal with the aftermath: the broken dream of a family and the lost hope of happily growing old together.

In my mind the situation could have been resolved with work from both of us. I still carry that disappointment today (even though Michael has passed away), and my heart aches for the real victims, Nae and Tee, for being innocently thrown into a situation they didn't deserve, and the impact it has had on their lives, even into adulthood.

Finding out her daddy wouldn't be coming home hit Naeaidria hard. They had the kind of relationship that kept me wondering how a love could be so strong. She and her wild imagination would have him cooking with plastic food (sometimes real food), dressed up for a tea party, playing with her make-believe friends, and babysitting her dolls. While in Germany, he took us on an adventure every weekend.

I struggled with helping Nae understand that our family now consisted of her, her sister, and me. At the beginning, she was angry, blaming me for the divorce. Tyresia was only two and a half, and really hadn't had a chance to get to know her dad.

The girls and I were eventually able to move on to a new normal. I was fortunate to have a good job, but it wasn't enough to take care of us. I'd grown tired of holding Michael accountable for his responsibilities, so I ended up working two other part-time jobs to make up for the lost income. My parents kept the girls while I worked and finished college for a better opportunity to provide for us, and God's mercy saw us through with my income and my family's support.

My parents took us under their wings. We needed them, and we were good for them as well. We did almost everything together. My house was the place we went to change our clothes, but we pretty much stayed with Daddy and Mother unless Daddy threw us out jokingly (I think), asking, "Y'all here again? Don't y'all have a house?"

Our family dynamics were different, but we were usually comfortable with the way things were. That expectation of the standard family structure made up of father, mother, children, and a pet, slowly decreased. Attending school events by myself was still hard.

One day Tee came home announcing that her teacher told her she didn't have a normal family. I never expected to have to explain to my five-year-old that some people aren't able to see anything beyond their own situation. I explained to her that there was nothing wrong with our family: we were together and cared for, loved, and looked out for one another. That's the definition of a family. She said she wished her family was like her friends' families, because "They have a daddy and I don't."

That was a hard one for me. After composing myself, I told her that she was fortunate to have both her father and her Pa-Pa (my daddy), because if it weren't for her father she wouldn't exist, and without her Pa-Pa life would be harder. She went away smiling about having a daddy in two different people.

Four years later, I was singing at a friend's wedding and met Joshua Hart. Joshua lived and worked in Northwest Arkansas. We began a long-distance relationship, which I'd never experienced before. We enjoyed getting to know each other by telephone for some time, then he invited me to come to NWA for a visit.

I was very nervous and didn't know anything about Northwest Arkansas. I didn't realize I had made a mistake in my travel arrangements until I was reading Joshua the directions, and all the names were Native American names. I remember him saying to me, "I have never heard of any of those places before."

I kept on reading until I got to the end of the email and read "Apache, Arizona." He cracked up and told me to call the airline right away. I had never been to either Arkansas or Arizona, so I didn't have a clue. The airline representative kindly told me how often this same mistake happens, and had no problem taking care of it.

Joshua also visited Port Arthur a few times during our short courtship before coming to talk to my Daddy about marrying me and moving us from Texas to Northwest Arkansas (NWA). I was hesitant in the beginning because I wanted him to guarantee that we would be together forever, but he has always been brutally honest. He said, "I will do my best, but in life there are no guarantees."

I've thought about that conversation often; he spoke the truth to me even though he knew that wasn't what I wanted him to say.

We spent Thanksgiving together with my family, which became our tradition. Our plan was to move during the holidays so that we could get Nae and Tee registered at school with as little disturbance as possible. I'd secured a job with J. B. Hunt, so everything was falling right into place. We left the Sunday after Thanksgiving, in a Penske moving truck with my car on a trailer, and drove the twelve hours to NWA.

We were both mature enough to prioritize things, and saving money to purchase a house took precedence over a big traditional wedding. When Joshua was able to leave work on Monday, we went to the courthouse and were married. Tuesday morning Naeaidria and Tyresia were both enrolled in their new schools.

Joshua had already been attending church in Bentonville, so we joined him for worship there. We had a hard time adjusting, but we began settling into our new life a little at a time. I felt fortunate to be living this life: a new marriage, a new residence, and a new job.

The last of my children was born when I was thirty-eight years old. I found out I was pregnant going into the eighth week. My only symptom was low abdominal pain, but when I went to see the doctor, test results showed without question that I was pregnant. This was considered a high-risk pregnancy due to my age, hypothyroidism, and other medical issues.

The doctor's office had closed for the day, and I had to get home for the second half of my work day: cooking, laundry, cleaning, and getting as much done on the endless list as possible. I drove home from the doctor's office after going through every human emotion—happy, sad, excited, and scared—in about two minutes.

I didn't know how I was going to break the news to my husband, fourteen-year-old, and eight-year-old.

This pregnancy was a real shocker and not in our ten- or fifteen-year plan, but it was a fact. I came in and started dinner a little later than usual, we all sat down to eat, and I just said it: "I just left the doctor's office, and I am going to have a baby."

Joshua said, "What, you're pregnant?"

I answered, "Yes."

After only a few bites, Naeaidria said she was finished eating and needed to get some homework done. Tyresia said, "Moma, are you going to be okay?"

I told her, "Yes, but we will have a new baby." She made it known that she didn't care for that, no doubt because she'd been the "baby girl" for so long.

The pregnancy was smooth now that I knew what was going on. My blood type is A-negative, so the Rh factor issue had to be addressed with extra bloodwork and an immunoglobulin injection. The obstetrician also wanted to do an amniocentesis to identify the developmental abnormalities that they were sure all of my issues would cause. We decided that wasn't necessary, because the baby would be ours whether there were problems or not, and God controlled that anyway.

The baby's position was breech as my due date approached. The doctor decided to manually turn her, but she would turn right back to feet first. I told my mother what was going on (she is always there when her grand-babies are born), and she decided to go ahead and schedule her flight. At my next appointment my doctor turned the baby again, and we were told to go straight to the hospital so they could induce me. My mother stayed with me, and Joshua left to drop the girls at home to get ready for school the next day, since we were told it would be some time before things got rolling.

I delivered Diana while Joshua was walking back into the hospital.

Joshua was so very excited. The doctor gave Diana to him, and I asked what we were going to name her. Throughout my pregnancy Joshua had convinced himself and me that I was having a boy. The doctor stood close to him and said, "You have a baby girl," but he still chanted, "My boy, my boy, my baby boy."

I asked Joshua again, "What will you name your baby girl?"

He put down his head and looked down at her again in his arms, and said, "She is a princess."

I said, "Well, I can't think of a princess name right now."

But he said, "Oh, I can: Diana. She will be Princess Diana." He gave her the middle name "Ngozi" after his sister. Her name is from his native country, Nigeria, and means "blessing."

We were so very fortunate; we received so many gifts that we didn't have to buy anything for a long time. My mother stayed with us for a couple of weeks and then returned to Port Arthur.

Diana was the center of attraction and attention. She was a very feisty little girl. I remember saying to Joshua and Naeaidria many times that it was okay for her to cry sometimes, but as soon as they heard her squirming in her bed, they would run off to get her. She definitely favored Joshua and Nae over Tee and me. There were many times that I couldn't settle her down no matter what I did. Then Joshua would take her and sing to her, and she would calm down immediately. Nae would just look at her and she would light up.

I had the opportunity to stay home with Diana a good amount of time before having to return to work at the Veterans Administration Medical Center in Fayetteville. I love being a mother; it is the most challenging job I've ever had. I hadn't had an infant for some time, and every child is different, so I was starting over.

When I went back to work, I would drop the older girls off at school in Bentonville every morning before dropping Diana off with a private sitter in Fayetteville. She took great care of Dee, and everything was going very well.

One Thursday morning, following my normal routine, I had parked and walked into my office building when I realized I had left my briefcase in the car. I went out to get it, and on my way back into the building, I encountered an F150 pickup truck: another employee was focused on a parking space and never saw me. My body sustained cervical, lumbar, and pelvic injuries requiring neck and back fusion. I was told the damage was caused not by the truck hitting me but from my body plummeting to the ground from the air.

Most of the next two years I spent in surgery or physical therapy, or at home recuperating and waiting for the next procedure. Finally, I was able to go back to work. I started on a schedule of four hours per day, but was in a lot of pain. The pain intensified until I couldn't stand it anymore. The surgeon thought I would benefit from a pain management doctor, but his numerous attempts to help didn't do much good. I saw the surgeon several times, and he was confident that the fusions in both my neck and back were solid. He said that my body had withstood a tremendous amount of trauma, and that I had developed a degenerative disc disease with a considerable amount of scar tissue. I also had back issues that had developed while in the military.

The surgeon thought the best thing for me was to focus on living the best I could with the pain. It was touch and go for a long time, but I did get to a point that I was able to function. During that time I was able to enjoy some of the school programs and organizations that the girls were involved with.

I finally had to take medical leave. This caused a huge void in my life, because I had worked since age sixteen, and work gave me a sense of identity. Without a "real" job, I struggled with my self-worth. I was a good cook, housekeeper, and classroom mom, and volunteered as much as I could, but it never seemed enough, yet I was limited because of the pain. I had a hard time altering my life yet again.

A lot of this was due to the way my father taught us to be self-sufficient. I never had the luxury of having anyone take care of me. The Lord made sure both Michael and Joshua were good providers, but I carried my load. I know now that I did not understand my worth. I realize today that I could have reached for higher goals, but I sold myself short. This is huge, because it affords me the opportunity to speak to young ladies, including my daughters, about having it all when you have defined what "all" is.

My definition of "all" was what I saw growing up. Daddy married Mama, they had children, they went to work. Our work was school until we were able to work to make money. We worked hard at being the best we could be in that job, and that is where the cycle would begin again.

I am afraid I handed the same things down to my girls. Both Nae and Tee saw me go to work, and work very hard for us to survive. They know my work ethic by the example I lived. They saw me define my strength by very seldom depending on anyone, even during times when we could have benefited from some help, but I didn't ask because I thought it was a sign of weakness. I don't hold my parents completely responsible, because I've made my own choices; however, they did define a lot of the way I view things.

Life moved us forward: Nae graduated high school and went on to Belmont University, nine hours from home. Being so far apart was tough on all of us, but again we all settled down to another "new normal." Tee went on to eighth grade, and Diana started school.

Joshua moved his brother and his family in with the four of us. Felix, his wife Doris, and their four kids joined us from Aba, Nigeria, and overnight we became a family of ten. This more than doubled the cooking, cleaning, and laundry, on top of all that goes into combining two very different families. But I was excited, because it gave me something to focus my energy into.

Their youngest (then eighteen months old) has Down syndrome, so I spent a lot of time getting her into places that provided services to help her thrive. Some of my time was spent helping both parents find work, after helping them both obtain their driver's licenses. I really felt like my life had purpose again, but it wasn't easy on any of us, particularly Diana. She was fortunate to have playmates her own age in our home now, but my time was being divided very thin. She wasn't used to having my attention pulled so many other places.

The time came for my brother-in-law to move his family into their own place, not too far away. We resumed more normal family lives, sharing plenty of family time together for the cousins to play. I am intentional about living in peace, and I worked tirelessly at keeping my family together. Celebrating birthdays, anniversaries, graduations, large Saturday morning breakfast, and sitting down together for Sunday lunch after church are my favorites. Really, any reason we can find to be together has been extremely important to me. I was so very thankful for my family and the life God had blessed me with.

Like many, I took a lot of things for granted. Unintentionally, good habits seem to just gradually change. I've since learned to pay attention to the fact that when things are going well, I am easily distracted, and it is hard for me to keep my prayer life healthy and make sure I am spending time with God by reading His Word.

IN SEARCH OF A DIAGNOSIS

A diagnosis of neuromyelitis optica (NMO) is made after a detailed patient history, a thorough clinical evaluation, identification of characteristic physical findings, and a variety of specialized tests. Such tests include but are not limited to blood tests, spinal tap and examination of cerebrospinal fluid, and a series of MRIs. The NMO-IgG blood test is highly specific and moderately sensitive for neuromyelitis optica. It has been shown to detect antibodies that are specific for an astrocyte protein, aquaporin-4. It is very helpful to request this test at the first significant suspicion of neuromyelitis optica, as it is frequently positive at the time of the very first symptom, long before a confident clinical diagnosis. Successful diagnosis of neuromyelitis optica depends on distinguishing it from MS. –National Organization for Rare Diseases (NORD)

I had been to my primary physician several times for some bizarre symptoms that had begun to concern me. After some standard lab testing, he was determined to get to the bottom of things, since the tests were all inconclusive. He decided to consult with a neurologist, but before I could be scheduled, I ended up in the hospital for an unexplained optic neuritis that caused permanent loss of the central vision in my right eye. It worked out that the neurologist was able to see me while I was inpatient. The treatment for optic neuritis is a five-day course of high-dose IV steroids, and in most cases some of the vision returns. But in my case, none of my vision returned.

Most neurological diseases are diagnosed by a process of elimination. The neurologist was leaning towards sarcoidosis, a disease characterized by the growth of tiny collections of inflammatory cells in some part of the body. However, in his initial exam I didn't present with a rash that is a common symptom of that disease. He told me not to worry, that he would continue the search until he had a proper diagnosis. After three days of inpatient treatment, I was released without improvement of my symptoms.

I saw an ophthalmologist as well, and he said at this point the loss of vision was permanent. I was scheduled for a follow-up appointment the next week with the neurologist who treated me while in the hospital. At that appointment I went through another series of tests, including a nerve conduction study that showed significant nerve issues.

After the major known neurological diseases were eliminated, I was mis-diagnosed with muscular sclerosis (MS) and began treatment in late 2009. I couldn't tolerate the initial medication, so we went through several more until the neurologist found one I did well on. However, the symptoms continued, and I began experiencing some new and different symptoms not typical of MS. I was told not to worry because stress actually aggravates the episodes, and every patient's case is different. I saw that neurologist a couple of times more, but then he retired, and my medicine was managed by my primary care provider until I found myself at the mercy of a new neurologist, Dr. Balmukund.

I was uptight at my initial visit with Dr. Balmukund. After all I had gone through to this point, it felt like I was starting all over again. However, he quickly put me at ease. He had read my records, reviewed all of the tests and MRI's before my appointment, and said he found my case very interesting.

This was a new experience for me, because most doctors take one look at my medical records and decide to let me tell them what the records say. He told me he was going to continue the current treatment over the next two months to give my body a chance to respond to the medication.

At the next appointment, Dr. Balmukund told me he had moved to NWA from the Mayo Hospital in Rochester, and had learned about a disease called neuromyelitis optica (NMO) just before he left. My condition was continuing to worsen, with new and confusing symptoms. He thought we should explore the possibility of my having NMO. At the time, NMO was believed to be a variant of MS, but it has been scientifically proven since then that NMO is a rare neurological disease separate from MS.

Dr. Balmukund decided to order the specific blood test NMO-IgG, which came back positive for NMO. It was now 2011, and for the first time in three years, I had the answer to all my unexplained symptoms. I remember the somber look on Dr. Balmukund's face at my next appointment. He is a very straightforward doctor, which I really appreciate. He told me he had been hoping that the results wouldn't be positive, because NMO was so newly discovered, with little to no knowledge about the disease, let alone a treatment. He gave me a paper about NMO that he had printed, and told me he was sorry.

Once again he put me at ease by telling me he would consult with his colleagues, and we would take it one day at a time and get through this together. He prescribed medication for the uncontrollable spasms I was having, as well as a different pain medication, and discontinued the medication for MS. He scheduled another appointment and told me to bring my family with me.

We went to that appointment together and listened to what he told us, but we were not really connecting his words to the situation. By now we were all aware of the uncontrollable spasms deforming my extremities, and the fact that I could be walking one moment and collapse to the ground the next. But in our minds, this was still not serious enough to talk about death. I managed to verbalize, "Don't just hand us a printout and say, 'I'm sorry.' There has to be something we can do."

After consulting with the Mayo Clinic, he did have a plan, which we started right away. He cautioned me not to worry, that it would take some time before we would see some change, but he was confident that things would get better. I was somewhat stable with no new symptoms, but I continued struggling with the pain and spasms. The plan was to treat the symptoms using high-dose steroids every other month to minimize the spasms, as well as to prevent new symptoms.

The next time I saw Dr. Balmukund, I'd started having a sensation like a band tightening around my waist, along with heaviness in my legs. He changed my medication to Rituxan, a form of chemotherapy that was showing good results for some patients with NMO. After some lab work, I started a six-hour infusion of Rituxan the following week. He warned me that this medication was not a proven treatment, but worth a try until something else became available. We took one long deep breath, then began cautiously breathing a normal pattern that lasted just long enough for us to feel like we had our normal life back again.

CUT FROM A DIFFERENT MOLD

My Mother Ethel's Witness

Timesia always did things her way. We would show and tell her exactly what to do, yet she'd manage to go ahead with her way. I would give my husband, John, a report every day when he'd come in from work, and he would brace himself for Timesia's report because it was always the longest. Much prayer over her life is what has gotten us this far. I love all my children, but Timesia was cut from a very different mold, and we worked overtime to bring her around.

I'll never forget the phone call from Timesia after church one Sunday evening. She said, "Mother, I just want to thank you for bringing me up the way you did, and for the loving way you have taken care of our family. Mother, know my great love for you."

This was July, during her second exacerbation, which was much more severe than the first one. Timi said, "Mother, I really believe this disease is going to take me out."

27

My immediate response was, *I don't how, but I am out of here now*. I needed to get to my daughter.

John said, "Why do you have to go? There is nothing you can do that the doctors are not already doing," but he knew he was talking to a brick wall, because I was going.

I called my daughter Sherida and told her to get me to Arkansas. I told her what Timi had said, and she had her husband, Rollin, book me on the next flight. Sherida and I met up at the airport in Little Rock, and went to the hospital where Timesia was.

When she saw us she was very upset—she didn't want anyone there. She was hooked up to so many different machines, and her breathing was very labored. We spent the night with her in the hospital, in those uncomfortable chairs. No one expected us to stay, and I was having leg cramps, but none of that mattered. I wasn't leaving.

When the doctors came in early the next morning, they made a decision to put her on a ventilator to rest her body. My daughter screamed like I never heard before for me to keep them from venting her. She said, "Mother, I will never survive. Please Mother, help me stay alive."

My mind and body went into shutdown mode, and I did what was familiar to me: I just cried out to God, asking Him to help us. Both Sherida and I were in tears, unable to speak. Joshua, Timesia's husband, was quiet as he usually is, but he had a look of fear on his face that I'd not seen before.

I called one of the members of my church, and she

reminded me that God was in control, and we needed to trust Him. I knew this, of course, but it was very hard. This was one of my children. The human being was so afraid, but the spirit being took control, and after we prayed, a spirit of gratitude came over me. Exhausted, we fell asleep.

I woke up to see a strange-looking man who said he knew what was going on, but not to worry about anything, just trust in God, everything was going to be all right.

Not long afterwards, the doctor came in to tell us that they had decided to wait until a plasmapheresis treatment was completed to see if there was a change in Timesia's condition before putting her on the ventilator. We hadn't been able to see her since they transferred her to the ICU, but the doctor said they were going to let us in after the treatment, once her vital signs stabilized. When we were allowed in, she was still struggling to breathe with little to no change, and fear began to creep in again; but the peace of God overpowered that fear.

Treatment after treatment over the next four days, all the while watching my daughter struggle to breathe, was difficult. We kept speaking the word of God over her and the situation, but the days grew cold and hard. What could we do when the specialty doctors didn't know what to do?

We loved on her, keeping her comfortable, washing, combing, and braiding her hair. She had been there two weeks before we made it there, and needed some tender loving care. Doing for her took my mind off my own pain and agony.

I am so thankful for Jesus, because He kept me during that time.

Finally I'd stayed as long as I could; it was time for me to go back to Texas. I wanted to take my granddaughter Diana back with me to make things easier for Joshua, but he wouldn't allow me. We had no idea how long it would be before things would get better, or for that matter if things would improve at all, but he said he would take care of Diana.

One month after I went back home, the decision was made to move Timesia to a nursing facility because she wasn't making progress. That heaviness came over me again—my daughter in a nursing home? No way. I was on my way back to Little Rock.

Joshua picked me up from the airport and took me straight to the hospital. When I saw my daughter, it took everything I had to keep from passing out. Her body was limp, frail, and very small.

As soon as she saw me, she asked me to stand her up, and at first I was happy because I felt like she was still fighting. I had no clue how bad she really was. I went to get her up and she was weak all over, much worse than before. I finally convinced her that we might end up breaking a bone or something if we kept trying to stand. I made her comfortable and thought we'd finally get some rest. I'd traveled all day, it was close to midnight, and I was tired.

Two minutes later Timi started crying and asking me

the tough questions for which I had no answers. She said, "Mother, what in the world is going to happen?"

I told her that we were going to continue to do what we'd always done: pray and trust God.

That was not the answer she was looking for. She came right back with, "Mother, our lives are to honor God. Please tell me how my mangled-up body is going to give glory to God?"

Very firmly I said, "There is nothing else we can do."

That was a very long night, but one I'll never forget. We sang and prayed for hours. At some point we both went to sleep. I was awakened when the nurse came in to inform us that it was time to leave—the discharge orders had been signed and forwarded to the nursing facility. By now Timesia was awake and very upset as reality set in. That nurse had the least amount of compassion or concern that I've ever seen. She had two clear plastic bags and began just cramming Timi's things into them.

But God has a way of taking care of His children, leaving no question that He is in control. He blessed us with the kindest discharge doctor from the UAMS Neurology Department; she took my daughter's limp hands and told her that her road to recovery would be long and hard, but to work hard, because she was confident that Timesia would get better. She was careful not to make promises about how much function would return, but she gave us hope that things wouldn't remain as bad as they were.

Off we went to the Concordia nursing facility, 220 miles

north in Bella Vista, Arkansas. Upon arrival, the staff met us with such warm greetings. They treated us like royalty. They directed Joshua where to park, and carefully transferred Timesia out of the car into a wheelchair. Before we could come in with her belongings, they had already processed her into her room. I'm talking straight VIP service.

I was going along with the program for now, but I had decided without talking to anyone that there was no way I was leaving my daughter in a nursing facility in Arkansas. But God—He flooded me again with peace that I still can't explain. This was a nursing facility where most people's physical therapy consisted of walking ten steps with their walker, or pushing themselves in a wheeled chair to the dining facility. The therapist wasn't sure what she was going to be able to accomplish with Timesia, but I knew that Timi would take advantage of every half of a chance to improve.

My heart ached for my daughter. She had truly dedicated herself to living out God's plan for her life, and it seemed as though this plan wasn't fair. I watched as her joy turned into sorrow. She wasn't able to do anything for herself. She has always been a fighter, but there seemed to be no fight left. She'd stare for hours, and when she talked, it usually ended up with her sobbing that she couldn't understand what God was doing. Again and again the question: "Mother, how can I glorify God the way that I am? I don't understand, it doesn't make sense."

Having no real answers broke my heart, and I prayed so

hard for God to give me something to say to my daughter. My heart ached for Joshua, as he worked, took good care of Diana, and then in the evenings after work came to take care of Timi. We tried everything we could to cheer her up, but nothing did.

Sherida came to take me back home. She had all kinds of cheerful decorations to put in Timesia's room, and Timesia had a fit. She told her sister to take it all back, that this was not a permanent situation, she did not want to get comfortable, because she was not staying. My daughter's personality changed. She was angry, and she took it out on everybody.

I was so happy one day when I went back after shopping, cooking, and cleaning, to see that her primary care doctor (Dr. Byrum) and his wife Susan, who was also Timi's friend, were visiting. I thought, *This will cheer her up*. We all ended up crying, praying, and seeking God's response.

After they left, I got her ready for bed and left to get myself some rest. When I came into her room the next morning, she said, "Mother, please help me stand up."

I said, "Let me get somebody to help me."

But she said, "Mother, just try, me and you."

I knew her strong will, so I just went over to stand her up. She stood up for one minute, and from that moment on she was on her way to recovery. The joy of the Lord filled her up again.

My time once again was spent, and I returned to Port Arthur.

BATTLING NMO

F inally getting a diagnosis confirmed what the severity
of my pain and weakness had been telling me: this was
something serious. Now the initial battle of getting a proper
diagnosis shifted to the battle to win my life back.

The first couple of times around (with two months or
so in between), things weren't so bad. I didn't know what
was happening with the first exacerbation, since I wasn't
even diagnosed yet. After the diagnosis, and by the second
exacerbation, I did start to worry.

I responded to the treatment initially, so my stay in the
rehab hospital was short. After treatment, in rehab therapy,
and in outpatient physical, occupational, and speech
therapy, I slowly began to regain strength. The process was
slow because my body was completely weak (a nice way
of saying paralyzed from my upper stomach to my feet).

Then I had a major exacerbation that paralyzed me, and
I was sent to UAMS in Little Rock. I've never felt so scared
and defeated as I was when my body went down. My mind

raced from one thought to another while I laid in bed month after month.

After the private pity party, I reminded myself of how I got this far. I thought about the times I should have been dead, but here I was alive still. I pulled together every ounce of courage I could find in my body and chose to do battle.

I was treated poorly every single time I ended up at a different facility, except for the nursing home. Many times the battle was for basic common decency, as if I needed one more struggle. One of the toughest battles on that front was in the hospital. I was alone, helpless, and completely at the mercy of those taking care of me.

I don't want to dwell on this, but take a minute and let yourself imagine how a paralyzed person might be mistreated. Everything that just came to your mind probably happened to me while in the hospital. I did not complain, because I did not want to be labeled "the bad patient" and get even more of the same inhumane treatment, but I'll share one of those stories now.

The hospital has procedures for patient baths. I was scheduled on Tuesday, Thursday, and Saturday. I always looked forward to getting cleaned up, but one day I was told I wouldn't be getting a bath because there was a shortage of nurses. I asked the nurse on duty not to pass me over for my bath. I told her I didn't mind if it was 2:00 a.m., just please clean me up. She said she would see but could not make any promises.

I waited, and when she made her rounds around 2 o'clock, I asked her again. She was angry that I wasn't sleeping, and told me it would take her some time to get everything ready but she would be back. She came back with a white plastic board I hadn't seen before and put it on top of the bathing bed. She used the lift to take me out of the bed and dump me on that cold plastic board.

She began spraying me with ice-cold water. When I asked her to please warm it up some, she turned it off and started rubbing me as if she were sanding down a piece of wood. I started crying and asked her why she was being so rough. She said she wanted to make sure I was clean.

I couldn't believe what was happening, so I began crying out to God, asking Him to please help me. I prayed for the other patients and prayed about the shortage of nurses. Through my sobs of despair, I said, "God, please bless this nurse, please meet her needs."

I heard a sniffle and saw that the nurse was crying. I asked her if she was okay. She said that she was sorry and was blown away by my prayers. I told her that God was everything to me, and when things were rough, He was my refuge. As she finished cleaning me up, I felt a strong urgency to ask her about her relationship with Jesus. She said she didn't have one, and in the bathroom that night, this nurse accepted Jesus as her Savior.

Sadly, not every story ended up so positive. I'd been on both sides: I had taken care of many patients as a medical care provider, and had been a patient before, so I knew how patients should be treated. I still don't understand how things could have been so bad. Having a rare disease is terrible, but being mistreated for having the disease (as if I could do anything about it) was the worst.

I was convinced that my disease was a temporary situation, and every day I'd tell myself, *Everything will be back to normal tomorrow*. This went on for four months. It was very frustrating because my hands, legs, and the rest of my body looked totally normal, but I wasn't able to use them. I did everything the therapists told me to do, with no response from my body.

I was trying hard to keep a positive attitude, but I was scared of what looked like a hopeless situation. The only way I could sit up in the bed was to have pillows stacked all around me propping me up. The day I was able to open and close my middle finger on my left hand at the therapist's command was such an accomplishment we both cried.

Everyone wanted to see this thing turn around as much as I did, but there wasn't much evidence that it would. My body went against the "norm." For example, I am right-handed, but for whatever reason, the left side of my body responded more quickly and remains the strongest side of my body today. My right side feels heavy and functions awkwardly, and I have limited sensation.

The first line of treatment was high-dose IV steroids. That was followed by seven rounds of plasmapheresis, which ran my blood through a device to separate the plasma from the blood cells. The plasma (containing the antibodies that were attacking my own body) was discarded and replaced with another compatible fluid. This was all done through a surgically placed large-bore catheter so that all my blood could be removed, treated with plasmapheresis, and replaced over several hours. Finally, treatment ended with chemotherapy. I was then transferred back to the rehab hospital for therapy.

The physical weakness of my body worsened after each exacerbation, both outwardly and internally, and there was more severe, irreversible damage. NMO is completely unpredictable, and it is harder to recover after back-to-back exacerbations.

There was no response to the therapy, my body began to shut down, and the doctors were not as optimistic about the treatment anymore. Unexpected new problems made it extremely difficult to keep going. The pain was excruciating, and the spasms were constant, even on the strongest muscle relaxers, which also kept me sick to my stomach.

For the first time, my mental status was shaken. I tried to hold on by reminding myself of the promises of God. My weakness and the ineffectiveness of therapy combined to send me down a dark path, and my mind began to match my physical status: shut-down mode. I remember thinking, *Oh, so this is how it happens. I am going to lose my mind while I die.*

Finally, I slowly started to show signs of improvement. However, the insurance company decided that I wasn't recovering fast enough compared to the first recovery. They instructed the medical team to prepare me to live the rest of my life in a wheelchair controlled by a one-finger remote, since I only had the use of my thumb and middle finger on my left hand, and limited use at that. Insurance gave the medical team two weeks to accomplish the task of helping me be as independent as possible.

A sense of abandonment set in quickly. It was as if the world came to an immediate stop. This time there was no cheering, encouraging me to keep pushing forward. Instead, it was about me accepting this new way to live. I was really resistant and kept asking for more time, but I was quickly transferred to the spinal cord, traumatic brain injury, and stroke department of the hospital to learn how to live life in my current condition.

The staff all looked at me with such pity, it made me sick to my stomach. The doctor on the floor told me one morning on his rounds that the sooner I accepted that I would be in a wheelchair the rest of my life, the better I'd "fare off." Throughout this journey, the Lord helped me keep my mind and my spirit, and I quickly responded that I was never going to accept that I'd be in a wheelchair the rest of my life. They carried on with their mission, and I carried on fighting with my weapon of mass construction: prayer.

Two days before the time was up, the nurse came into my room to tell me the doctor was on his way in to see me. I started praising God, thinking the doctor was going to give me more time; but quite the contrary. That doctor came in to tell me they all agreed that I needed to be discharged already since I'd mastered all the skills I would be able to, and there was nothing else they could do for me.

"Release me to where?" I asked.

He said he didn't know, but that my next of kin (Joshua) had been notified to pick me up. Joshua was also told to find a facility for me, but he had no idea where to start.

I made contact with the Veterans Administration Medical Center (VAMC) and told them what was going on. Within a few hours, they had found me somewhere to go once released. I'd be going to Concordia Nursing Facility back in Northwest Arkansas.

I was so thankful that God had made a way, and I had somewhere to go. Joshua couldn't take care of me, and he did not want me to go back to Texas with my family. It wasn't until we arrived at the nursing facility that reality hit me: *I am here because they think I am going to die*.

I JUST NEED MY MOMA

My Daughter Diana's Witness

"My mother is so pretty, and she is so kind. She comes to see my activities at school, she tucks me into bed every night. I love my Mother. I wish my mother wasn't sick, because I need her here with me."

I read these words on one of Diana's writing pads after returning home from one of my many hospital stays.

Early in Diana's fifth grade year is when things started to change for all of us, because I was sick and in the hospital three hours away. The school was made aware of the situation, and they supported us every way they could. We are forever grateful for the many hands that helped us during this time.

Joshua had to continue working, plus he was in charge of everything from getting Dee ready in the morning to after school care and picking her up. When they got home in the evening, their routine was dinner, homework, bath, and bed, then wake up and repeat. I know what I was going through during this time, but I can only imagine what this little nine-year-old girl was going through. The reality is that everyone involved had no choice but to deal with what was happening in their own way.

* * *

I remember asking Mrs. Jenny why I had to go home with her, and when my mother was coming to pick me up. She told me she didn't know, but my daddy would be picking me up once he got off work.

He did, and we went right to the hospital. I ran to the bed where my Moma was, and asked her what was wrong and if she was coming home with us. She was very sad and didn't move very much, but she told me everything was going to be all right. I know now she didn't know what was going on, and as usual she wanted to make sure I didn't worry.

I didn't see my mother again until the following weekend, and we had to drive three hours to get to where she was. We were so glad to see each other. We talked on the phone every night and prayed before I got into bed, but it wasn't the same as being with her.

It was very strange, because Moma couldn't play with me. We always played games, and I had brought two of our favorites, but she couldn't move her arms and hands. She tried to explain what was happening, but it was hard for me to understand because she had been just fine a few days ago.

Moma and I talked about everything going on at school and church, but it was getting late and Daddy was tired, so we said goodbye and Daddy and I went to the hotel to sleep. The next day we were right back at the hospital to see Moma again. When we got there, they were taking her down to therapy, so we went with her. The therapist was helping her with exercises, but she wasn't doing them very well. She was having a lot of pain and spasms. I kept telling her to keep trying, that she would get it. We spent most of the day together, and then it was time for Daddy and me to get back home and get ready for the week.

It was always so hard to leave my Moma. I would cry on the ride back home until I fell asleep, and Daddy would wake me when we finally reached home.

Mrs. Susan and Mrs. Sandra helped us out the times we didn't go to the hospital. Mrs. Sandra always let me have lots of the good bacon, and Mrs. Susan always knew the best place to get the good yeast bread I like. My Nanny Rida, Nanny Cat, and MoeMoe (my aunts Sherida and Wanda and my grandmother) came often to help us out too. My sisters came home as often as they could, and that helped all of us, because we all had the same thing missing out of our lives: our mother.

I still spent a lot of time by myself. Moma and I were so close, but she wasn't here. I was lonely and sad. I remember everybody doing so many good things to help me, but things just weren't the same without my Moma.

It seemed like months and years went by before Moma was back home, and even then, she was so weak that we had to take care of her. I had to help her with her bath, her hair, and getting dressed. I had no choice but to grow up quickly, taking care of myself and doing what had to be done to help take care of my Moma.

I felt like I was alone even after Moma was home for good. I had a hard time readjusting after learning to live without her for so long, and now that she was getting better, it seemed like she was on my case for everything. Our relationship changed, I became rebellious, and we really drifted apart. I cannot explain it nor do I know exactly what happened; we just became distant.

I know now that there is no other human in this world who cares more for me than my Moma, and I am so happy she is doing better now. I have watched her fight to survive NMO, even when the doctors gave up on her. She made up her own exercises after each therapy session was over. She would fall often and dared any of us to help her up. Moma told us that unless she called out for our help, not to worry, and she very seldom asked for help.

For everything I went through, I am strong because of how I watched my mother's strength. I have been proud to follow in my mother's footsteps and serve in the United States Army. I am a long way from where I want to be, but I believe I will get there.

* * *

Having my youngest child go through this ordeal has left me with many unanswered questions, but I do know that she was my number one reason to fight for my life. I remember the night I stayed up all night praying to God about how He gave her to me. I reminded Him how she came into being, as if He needed reminding; but I felt like I was justified in asking Him to allow me to live at least long enough to see her graduate high school.

We found out early on that Diana is a social bug, which didn't go well for her when she was supposed to be doing any subject outside of reading, lunch, or P.E. I remember her coming home the first time the teacher had to talk to her about it.

She said, "Moma, Mrs. Smith said, 'Diana, you need to MYOB.'"

I asked, "Dee, what is MYOB?"

She said, "Mind your own business," which told me a lot about what was going on at school. I am an old-school Moma. Before any teacher tells me any truth about my child, I've observed it already at home.

Diana didn't lack attention; she had it whether she wanted it or not. Since she was the youngest child, we tried to get her to every event, and allowed her to participate in the things she wanted as long as it didn't interfere with her academics. We did our very best, and expected the same of Diana. She wasn't perfect, of course, but she always tried hard to do what was expected of her.

The interruption from NMO affected all involved, but Diana took a hard hit. Being so close to me, it was difficult for her all the time I was away, and my heart ached for her. Joshua had a lot on his plate and wasn't used to doing all the personal and household tasks. He did the best he could, but he wasn't me.

I know now that Diana had to grow up very fast. The visits back and forth were hard on her, especially during the dark days. Some of the things she would say just tore me up inside. One such time was a Sunday after she and Joshua had been with me at the University of Arkansas Medical Center in Little Rock for the weekend.

She always got really quiet when she knew it was time for them to go. She would lie in the bed with me, trying to stay as long as possible. I'd see her glance over at her Dad to see if she could tell when he was going to get up and say "Okay, it's time." Since she was very little, Diana had a habit of rubbing our arms, hands, or whatever skin she could find, which I think calmed her down. That day she rubbed and rubbed my arms and hands so much, letting me know she was feeling uneasy.

She kissed me and looked down at me and said, "Moma, why can't you just come home like you are?" (For weeks we had been telling her I needed to get a little bit stronger before I could come home.) "I don't want to go home and leave you here again, can you just come home?"

I had no words, and the tears began to well up in my eyes. I managed to say, "I'll work really hard this week, and maybe I'll be strong enough next time."

Joshua came over, picked her up out of the bed, kissed me, and told me he would call once they reached home. I thought this was the hardest thing I'd ever been through, but to think about the agonizing pain that my little girl was going through was awful. I cry-prayed until the phone rang and her voice came over the line. It was filled with happiness because Joshua had let her have a happy meal with medium fries. That made for a restful night for all of us.

I did come home eventually, but there were so many things to contend with, all of which I couldn't do anything about because my body was so weak.

We settled into a "new normal" again. Dee went to school and came home on the bus for the first time since starting school. Joshua went to work as usual, and I was home doing physical, occupational, and speech therapy. Dee and Joshua made dinner (she was so very eager to help with everything), but in my mind I wondered how she could do all of this. After all, she was just a little girl.

It wasn't very long before things operated like a well-oiled machine, but that was short-lived. The cycle repeated itself, and the second exacerbation proved more violent, with recovery seeming impossible.

At my final homecoming, I was greeted by a twelve-year-old who had been through a lot. She'd been influenced by her teachers (both at school and at church), our family, and friends helping out when they were needed, and very little by me. While recovering, I noticed how much Diana had changed. She was very opinionated and independent. She struggled with peer pressure and the issues that come along with it.

I tried helping her the only way I knew how, and that seemed to push her away. Our helpers during all that time had sympathy for her and allowed her to slack on her chores and homework. Joshua enforced the basic rules, but was lenient because of the situation. I knew what she was capable of, so no matter what was happening to me, I emphasized that she had to do her very best at all times, but she thought I was being mean.

I cried to God, reminding Him again how He had given Diana to us. During my prayer I realized that the only thing we could do now was give her back to Him, and I felt such relief. Things didn't change instantly, but I was ready for God to have His way in her life no matter what it meant.

I talk to Diana Ngozi Hart daily, and she knows that my prayer for her is that she would have the desire to seek God and develop a relationship with Him. I pray that He orders her steps, and where He leads her she will follow. I pray His goodness and mercy over all the days of her life. I give Him glory for allowing me life to see the transformation He is making in her life.

GOD IS STILL IN THE HEALING BUSINESS

My Sister Wanda's Witness

Our relationship is as bonded and as loving as sisters can be—solid as a rock. We talk three or four times a week, about everything: family, church, friends, our health, and our favorite topic: food.

What Timesia went through with NMO was scary. There were so many times I felt as if God was not answering or even listening to our prayers. I knew I had to remain strong and stay focused on being positive, and not allow the hurt, sadness, pain, and disappointment to show.

I coped by watching Timesia stay prayerful. She never gave up. Her commitment to herself made me want to focus and fight three times harder than she was having to. She was the victim; I was just a bystander, waiting for something to happen.

I learned the true meaning of "a family that prays together stays together." I learned that God is still in the healing business. Most of all, I learned how strong my sister's faith in God is. She never let us forget where all her blessings come from.

I encourage other people by telling my sister's story. When her doctor gave up on her, God said, *Wait, not yet.* Codes were called on her, but again God said, *Hold up now, she ain't ready yet.* My sister did her own therapy so she could use her hands, legs, arms, and body again. I don't feel like I did very much, but what I did, I would gladly do again if needed.

* * *

My sister Wanda—we call her Kitty—is the one I always wanted to look like. She may be "the baby," but she is the hardest-working of us all. She is dependable, knowledgeable, and will give 110%.

The first time she came to see me in the hospital, I was so happy; at that time we were optimistic that everything would be fine. She had been keeping up with the situation by phone, but she said she had to come see things for herself. She was convinced that I was going to be okay.

The next time she came, she didn't tell me she was coming, and I was upset because I didn't want her to know that things weren't going well. This was my second time in the hospital. We had spent July 4th together, and by the end of the month I was paralyzed again.

She knows me very well, so she just came right on in and went to work. I needed to be properly cleaned, and my hair needed to be shampooed and combed. I had been lying in that bed for weeks, and my beautifully conditioned skin had begun to break down. It was dry, scaly, and patchy, but my sister moisturized it back to its normal self.

We follow Mother's example when it comes to keeping our bodies from head to toe. No matter what is going on, Mother's hair is right, her face is made-up, and every piece of clothing is properly positioned to complement her body. Kitty had a lot of work to do on me that day. I cried all day; first of all because she did it so lovingly, but most of all because she had to do it. I deserved to be properly cleaned, and have my hair brushed at least once a week, but unless my family came, it didn't happen. I understood the hospital staff's focus, but being taken care of made such a difference.

I also needed a few good meals. My muscle mass was down, if I was going to ever walk again, I needed to increase it. I couldn't feed myself, and I was on the spinal cord injury floor where there were a massive number of patients but so few nurses they couldn't get around to everyone who needed feeding, so I'd only have a few bites at each meal.

Kitty made sure I ate all I wanted, waiting patiently until I slowly chewed each bite before giving me another one. She allowed me to cry, ridding myself of the emotional strain of being strong for my husband, my mother, my girls, and everyone else, and feeling as if this was my fault. Her support was such a necessary relief.

After Kitty left that Sunday, I felt restored. Mentally, I had emptied myself of so much guilt and defeat, and was recharged with a positive attitude and determination to persevere. I was back on track thanks to her TLC.

Kitty was also the energizing battery that charged us after the transplant. She stepped in to relieve Rida, following every detail of the doctor's orders. When problems presented, she took care of them immediately. Life can throw you around, and Wanda Marie Minniefield is an example of how you fight to win. This sister and I have many of Daddy's traits: we are both strong, and even when we don't have what we need to win, we win with what we have.

HOW DO I HELP MY MOMA?

My Daughter Naeaidria's Witness

I am so proud that Timesia, the strongest woman I know, is my mother. Anyone who knows me knows my mother. She has always had my back. She is my best cheerleader; out of nowhere she will call and speak life into me.

We have so many things in common. My mother introduced me to Jesus. I appreciate music because of my mother's enthusiasm for music; she gave me my voice. I am who I am because of my Mother pouring all she could into us. Her love is rare, unique, a beautiful display of the love of Jesus.

After graduating college, I stayed in Nashville to pursue my career. I had a role in a play that opened on my mother's birthday weekend. She decided to visit for the weekend and brought my sisters to Nashville to see the show. The entire time I was on stage, I kept looking at her wondering, *What's wrong with my mother?*

After the show we all came home to eat and visit with friends, but Moma had a headache and complained of her neck being stiff. The next morning, she went to the store, picked up groceries, and cooked all of us breakfast. We rested until Moma and my sisters had to get on the road.

We talked as usual when they arrived home, and Moma said she was tired and her neck was still hurting.

My high school classmate Christian called me up that Thursday, after Moma went home. She said, "Nae, your mother is in the hospital, and it doesn't look good."

I called, but it was some time before I finally reached Moma to find out what was happening. She told me they didn't know what was going on, and that she was being transported to Little Rock, but not to worry; she would let me know as soon as they knew something. I started making plans immediately to get to Little Rock.

I called the rest of my family to see if anyone knew what was going on, but at the time I was the only one, so I relayed the message Moma gave me to everyone else. It was strange that no one knew what was happening, but it was intentional: that is Moma's way of keeping everyone from worrying. It doesn't work.

After we all talked, Nanny Rida and Nanny Cat (Moma's sisters Sherida and Wanda) and I all made plans to get to Little Rock by the weekend.

Once we were there, my younger sister Tyresia joined us. We spent the weekend joking and laughing like we always do when we are together. We were hopeful that this would all be over in a few days, but I was scared. Moma put on a good act, but I watched the way she sat propped up in the bed, and how we had to pick her up to get her to the bathroom.

Eventually we all left, hoping for good results from the lab tests. The doctors on call that weekend told us that once the results were in, they would know what to do.

We managed to talk throughout the week, and by the following weekend, we all knew that this wasn't going to be a quick in-and-out situation. Moma's condition was worsening, and there were still questions as to the right treatment, because she wasn't responding to any of the medications.

My Dad and my baby sister Diana went down to Little Rock from Bentonville, and that was good for all of us, but there was little change in Moma's condition. The neurologist said that the next thing they were going to try was plasmapheresis, which would require inserting a line into Moma's neck (a surgical procedure). When Daddy told us, I made arrangements for my MoeMoe (my grandmother) to be there, since Daddy had to work and take care of Dee in school.

This was the start of my dilemma. I wanted to leave the school where I was employed and come home. I felt I should be the one there for my Moma. Some of the family thought I was wrong for not being there, but my parents both told me that I was going to stay in Nashville and live my life—that this was not my issue.

I was so torn. It was hard to focus, knowing my Mother was so ill. I don't know how I did it, but I wanted to be obedient, so I stayed in Nashville and went back home when I could.

It wasn't long until Moma was being prepared to go to rehabilitation. The plan was for her to continue treatment while getting back on her feet. At that point, things seemed to be turning around. We continued taking turns going home to help out with Diana and going to Little Rock to see Moma.

We were all excited the day Daddy picked Moma up from Little Rock. She was weak and in a wheelchair, but we knew Moma would do her best to get stronger and out of that chair. With home health nurses and a therapist, Moma was walking with a walker the next time I was home. I told her I would be glad to come home and help out again, but she told me that things were going to be fine and that I needed to get on with my life, so I went back to Nashville.

School was out for the summer, so Dee would be home, and Moma was getting better and better, but I really wanted to be home. July 4th weekend came, and Nanny invited us to Dallas to celebrate. It was the first time Moma would be going out, and everyone was excited. Her favorite fish and salad were on the menu, and Nanny Cat did her feet and fingernails. Moma was still weak and unable to do small things, so we just loved on her as much as we could.

By that Thursday evening Moma was headed back to Little Rock because she had relapsed. We weren't worried because we thought we knew what we were up against, and we just came back together with our rotation plan and suited up to take care of things again. But this time was different. The weakness came on quickly and much harder than before, and goodness, none of her treatments were working.

The hardest thing for all of us was that we had the wedding of the year planned for my cousin Rolonda, and we all felt that Moma had to be there. Up until two days before the wedding, we were still hoping the doctors would at least let her out for the ceremony, but they wouldn't allow it. This was so hard on our entire family, especially Moma. I remember leaving the hospital with all of us in tears because she was so sick. We made it through that wedding on her prayers, but it was not easy.

The next time I saw Moma, she was in rehab in Fayetteville and doing better, and we celebrated my birthday. We were hopeful that she would be home for the holidays. It was our family's time to host Thanksgiving, and we all had so much to be thankful for. Moma came home and again worked really hard to recover. This exacerbation had been so severe that it was taking longer for Moma to get back on her feet. Moma goes hard at anything she does, so she wanted to cook and clean and work just as hard as she could.

We hosted Thanksgiving, and it was a blessing to have her home. But it wasn't long before the cycle repeated itself again. Each time it seemed harder to recover, and she never really got back to where she was before. When she was at the rehab center the third time around, we found out about an experimental transplant as a treatment, and began researching to find out how she could participate in a trial.

Moma and her team at the rehab center got specifics and sent an email, not knowing what to expect. A few days later the response came with the details. The requirements seemed like an impossible feat, but we were up against a brick wall, and the doctors offered little other hope for this cycle to end.

The first thing we were told to do was get Moma strong enough to be evaluated in Chicago, where the trial was being conducted. Moma was extremely weak from the previous exacerbation even before the third one came on, but she did get strong enough, and I took the trip to Chicago with her for evaluation.

The responsibility weighed heavily on me. Moma was still very weak and in critical condition because her immune system was so compromised from all the medication. At the same time, I was so proud that I could finally do something big for Moma by going on this journey.

I was not prepared for what we were going to go through. Prayer and relying on each other's strength was the only way we made it.

We had never been to an enormous medical center like Northwestern Memorial. Where we were staying was a few blocks away, too far for Moma to walk back and forth, so I had to wheel her there and back multiple times throughout the day to make all of her appointments. There were also a couple of appointments on another campus, so we had to take the railway to get there, and I had to figure out which one to take and how to get Moma on and off safely.

I was scared, concerned, and hopeful all at the same time. I had to learn things as they were happening. Moma is a control freak, so I had that to deal with, on top of keeping everything together to report back to the home team. It was all worth it. At the end of the fifth day, Dr. Richard Burt and his team came into our last appointment and told us that everything so far looked good, and someone would be in touch with us within the week. They gave us a ton of paperwork, and then we rested and flew back to Northwest Arkansas armed with a plan to do away with this cycle of disease.

God opened the doors for this opportunity, the doctors were on board with us, and we were excited to bring back all of what we learned. Quitting was never an option, but now we were finally armed to fight. We didn't know what that fight was going to look like, but we teamed up to do serious battle.

When I think about that time, I think about all Moma's stories of when she was in the Army. She really took being a soldier seriously, and we drew on that mentality. We had to rely heavily on each other, just as in the military. There were days that things were too tough for me, so I had to pull strength from another team member; and that is how you make it.

All of our lives have been altered by what we went through together. Moma says often that there isn't much any of us couldn't get through, because we are always right there going through it with each other. I am so thankful to be able to tell the story this way, because it could have turned out very differently.

* * *

Naeaidria (affectionately Nae) made me the happiest woman alive when I gave birth to her. I made all my mistakes as a new mother on her. I had some teenage experience babysitting my sister's children and any other children I could, but there is something different about your own child. Nae remains my go-to girl for so many things. She has always been honest, and wants the best for me.

There is no way that we would have survived without Nae's ability to stay focused. She has always been mission driven. I'll cherish forever the way she shielded me from harm on the first trip to Chicago. She'd be off somewhere to take care of something, and I'd think, *Did she leave me? When is she going to come back?* and then she'd appear and take me on to the next appointment.

Naeaidria continues to support me. She works alongside me with the Living to Win Foundation. Neuromyelitis optica took so much from me. I am not sharp intellectually,

I am unable to command my old voice range, and my body is frail and weak. One day as I was crossing the street, a man yelled out his window at me to go home and sleep it off, because I walk like I'm drunk. Nae reminds me of what I told her when she was little: "You can do anything you put your mind to. It may not be what it once was, but be happy for what you can do. To whom much is given, much is required."

I had more time and energy to pour into Nae because she was my first, but I don't take credit for who she is. She is so very strong and a blessing to our family.

HAVE YOU TALKED TO MOMA?

My Daughter Tyresia's Witness

I was born in Watertown, New York, but don't remember anything about it. I was raised in Texas—we moved there when I was nine months old, after Moma finished her military service.

I was the baby in the family for a long time. Nae was my big sister, and she was nice to me growing up. My MoeMoe and PaPa spoiled me, and Nae and I spent lots of time with them while Moma worked. I remember working on school projects, playing outside, going to church every Sunday, and family get-togethers.

We moved to Northwest Arkansas when I was eight. I picked up where I left off in Texas: school, chores, church, playing, and youth events in the summer—a pretty normal childhood. My mother and I were very close, and then Diana came along. Our family dynamics changed, and so did Mom, and my relationship with her. My life went on as the "middle child." I graduated high school, went to college, then on to a program to learn office skills. I was finding my way in life.

One day I answered my phone, and it was Nae, my oldest sister. Right away I could hear in her voice that something was wrong. She asked me if I had talked to Moma. Since I was in Hot Springs, there would be times when I didn't talk to Moma daily. When I did, she always wanted to talk mostly about my life, so I seldom knew what was really going on at home.

Before answering my sister, I thought about the last time I'd talked to Moma. It was earlier that week, and I didn't remember her mentioning not feeling well. Nae gave me a play-by-play, then said that Moma was being taken to UAMS in Little Rock by ambulance.

I couldn't believe she was that sick. We had all been together at Nae's show having a great time for Moma's birthday a week or so before. Before dropping me and my friend back at the program we were in, Moma had made sure I had everything I needed, like she always did. She had called as usual once she and Dee made it home, so finding out that she was so sick didn't make sense to me.

I was used to Moma having to go into the hospital from time to time, but she always came out the way she went in, as far as I could tell. I just told myself, *This is another one of those times Moma is sick, but she will be fine.* The time that immediately came to mind was when I was at a game, and ended up having to find my own ride home because (as I learned after I finally got home) Moma was in the hospital.

I wanted to get there to be with her as soon as I could, but the program I was in wouldn't allow an absence without a verified excuse, and that would take some time. Nae was in the same situation, so she understood. We talked for a little while longer, because now I was as upset and scared as Nae. We didn't know very much, so she told me to keep trying to call Moma's mobile phone when I could, and whichever of us talked to Moma first would fill the other one in.

Even after getting to the hospital and seeing things for myself, I couldn't believe how bad things were. Moma looked like herself but couldn't do anything. She was having painful spasms that came on without warning and then released as fast as they came on. Nanny Rida was there, and then Nae came, and all of us including Moma were thinking, *We don't know what this is, but it will be over soon and everything will be back to normal.*

We all had to be back by Monday, so we spent our time enjoying each other rather than being upset about what was going on with Moma. We took turns getting her to the bathroom, feeding her, and helping with whatever she needed. I didn't know any more when I left than I did before, but I was hoping that these issues would just go away.

We stayed in touch with each other from that point on, but there was no change for what seemed like forever. Moma had always bounced back, but this time was different; it was bad for so long. We didn't know what was going to happen. The day Nae called to tell me Moma was starting to control her hand, that it was starting to feel normal, I was so happy. The next thing I knew, Moma was being transferred to the rehabilitation center. I visited her again, and she continued to improve until she was released to go back home.

Those were the hardest months on all of us. It was hard to concentrate, but I did, knowing how important it was to Moma for me to finish my program and settle into my career. So many things happened without Moma that we will never be able to go back and do again, like my cousin Rolonda's wedding. We do everything as a family, and there was an obvious empty space with Moma not being there. We each had to pull our own load, as well as take care of the things Moma would have done.

Moma missed my graduation from the program. I stayed in Hot Springs a while, then moved to Jonesboro. In between moving, I went home right after the 4th of July weekend. Everyone had been traveling different places. My family had returned from visiting Nanny Rida in Dallas, and I was glad to be home.

It didn't take long to notice Moma wasn't feeling well: she was kind of dragging, and that isn't Moma at all. She called the neurologist on call at UAMS (it was after clinic hours), and explained what was going on. She was told to get to the hospital as soon as we could.

I helped her get some things together, put a small bag together for Diana and myself, and drove us to the hospital. Moma was admitted again, and the doctor started the IV medication right away. We were all hoping that the meds would work and Moma's time in the hospital would be short. That wasn't the case. This was a major episode, and Moma was down for much longer than before.

I was torn in two different directions. I wanted to be with my mother, but there were so many things going on in my life. I knew I had to step up and help my sister; she had been through so much during the first episode, and I hadn't been around. I was here now, so I did what had to be done. Dee and I had to get closer; Moma was down and Daddy was working, so we had each other to depend on and make it through. I was glad to be there, because Moma, not wanting to worry us, didn't always let us know how bad things were.

I went home as often as I could while she was in the hospital and when she was transferred to the rehabilitation center. We had some very special times together. I felt like I was doing for my mother what she has always tried to do for me, and things she needed that no one else could do at the time. It made me happy to be there when she needed me the most.

I was also able to go home when Moma was finally released, and it was like she was starting all over again, but she was always so positive. The one time I saw her discouraged was when she found out that there was no way to stop the episodes. It was heartbreaking. The recurring episodes were becoming hard to treat, because she had problems with the medications.

Just when things seemed to be too much, Moma told us about a trial that she was going to try to participate in that might be able to help. We were all so excited, and ready for things to get better.

After the transplant, Moma worked day in and day out to get back on her feet. I am so proud of how far she has come. It is unbelievable that there was a time not long ago that my Moma was dying. I was there when she was unable to stand, or even to bring a fork from the plate to her mouth because her hands and arms were so weak. To see her now thriving is a miracle.

* * *

Tyresia (Tee), my middle daughter, has always been my tender-hearted girl. When she was around four years old, a shy little girl, she would cry after being dropped off at daycare and need extra care until one of us would pick her up. She didn't mingle with the other toddlers. It was a good thing that we enrolled her in pre-school and she didn't have to stay there long. She did a little better in pre-school, but compared to my other girls, she needed more encouragement to play and make friends.

Eventually she broke out of her shell, and it was beautiful when she spread her wings to fly. Tee came in from school after moving to Northwest Arkansas, and told me something I'd told her many times: "In order to make friends, you have to be a friend." It was her way of encouraging me to get on with life. It was very noticeable to her that I was having a hard time fitting in. The culture was different; however, having lived in many different places in the Army, it was only a matter of time before I settled in.

Since she was so young when we moved to NWA, her daily activities were still pretty much like they had been in Texas. She went to school and church, played with friends, and got into arguments with her big sister Nae (who was always busy with extracurricular school activities). Tee and I were close too. I would tell her often, "Tee, don't ever change. Stay sweet and always be concerned for other people."

She would respond, "Moma, I am who I am and I will always be me."

Then the teenage years came, and I became "the worst mother in the entire world." For whatever reason, Tyresia thought of me as being against her, even though I am her biggest fan. Our relationship suffered somewhat, but things resolved once Tee realized that, like most parents, I only wanted better for her than I'd had.

As she entered her adult life, having to function as a productive citizen in this world, she found more clarity about why she was raised the way she was. I wanted to prevent my girls from having the painful experiences I had gone through because no one told me certain things.

When I went into the hospital and Tee came to see me, she came straight to the bed and started asking me what happened. I knew she had heard it from her aunt and sister, but she wanted me to tell her, so I did. I allowed her to get all of her questions out, and emphasized to her that we were going to be all right. She believed me until the uncontrollable spasms started and she witnessed the pain that came along with them. It was really hard for her to see that I was unable to move anything from my waist down.

I know how strong my girls are, and the three of them drew strength from each other. They collectively and separately strengthen me in their own ways. Any time I couldn't figure out how to do something electronically, Tee helped me. She showed me how to have my phone play Scripture because I was unable to hold my Bible. She set up my phone so that the nurses could turn on the app, and Scripture would play until either the phone needed to be charged or the section of Scripture finished. She knew how important the Word of God was to me, and knew it was important to help me keep my routine of studying Scripture.

Tee would sit and talk to me for hours, keeping me up to date with world and local news. She helped make appointments and arrangements to take care of the things Diana needed while I was both inpatient and in rehab.

The nurses would question her about all the things she was doing, because she is my shortest daughter and they thought she was a child. She did anything she could find to do, from feeding me to freshening me up and changing the bed. I would say to her, "Just sit down and let's talk," and she would say, "Moma, I want to do a few more things, then we can talk."

She made things comfortable for me when I came home after the worst exacerbation, and she was part of my care rotation after the transplant. I heavily relied on Tee to keep things going in the house when she came home. I am so very grateful for the way Tee stepped up, and feel like I took too much from her while I was very sick. I've shared that with her, and she said it was what she had to do and that she would do it all again.

I asked Tyresia what she would share with a daughter or son of a very ill parent, to help them get through what she endured. She said she just followed my example. She also put herself in her little sister's shoes, and did what she would have wanted someone to do for herself. She had friends helping her stay strong for me, and she prayed a lot.

I am so proud of my tender-hearted middle girl. There is no way I could be here today without her in my life.

DO SOMETHING!
WHAT ABOUT A TRANSPLANT?

The third major exacerbation wasn't as serious as the first two, but I'd reached a point of just wanting everything to be over. I had been in the nursing home, but I was transported to Mercy for stabilization before being transported back to UAMS in Little Rock.

On the way to Little Rock, one of the paramedics recognized me, as he had transported me on one of the many trips back and forth. While trying to calm me down with small talk, he asked why I was going all the way back to Little Rock for rehabilitation and treatment. I told him that I was familiar with the process and so was the majority of the staff on the medical rehab floor. I also explained that I had been told that the rehab center in Little Rock was one of the best.

He agreed, but also told me that he had just recently trained in Fayetteville at a rehab center that also received high reviews and would be only fifteen minutes away from home instead of four hours. He suggested I visit with their patient care coordinator when it was time to start rehab.

UAMS started the standard plasmapheresis treatment. Mercy hospital in Bentonville had already given me the initial treatment of IV steroids. The neurologist on call also ordered an MRI in the ER. Not long afterwards, he came into my room and confirmed new active lesions, both in my brain and spinal cord. I was still struggling after plasmapheresis, so Rituxan was ordered for the following day. This was the routine every time I had an exacerbation; then after treatment we would pray and wait for the symptoms to resolve so we could begin rehab again.

The waiting game is so tough, because there is no time frame for the body to respond. During that waiting period, my team continued to treat other symptoms that popped up. Each time around, my body was slower to respond to treatment, and this time was no different. Every organ in my body seemed to be affected this time. The neurological team were concerned about so many issues. This ordeal seemed like it was getting the best of us.

This was the first time I experienced severe respiratory problems. I was transferred to the intensive care unit, where the doctors were preparing to intubate me. I was alert enough to know what was going on, and cried for Joshua and Rida not to let that happen. I felt so strongly that I would never come off that machine. Later that evening my vitals and respiratory system started to improve, and I believe it was because of a breathing treatment that one of the respiratory specialists asked to do. After two more days the doctor released me to the step-down unit (with less intensive care).

I was on the medical side of the hospital for weeks before being transferred to the rehabilitation side. At that point I had a conversation with the patient care coordinator and asked if they would consider rehabilitation in NWA. She said that as long as the facility had an opening and would be able to follow the orders prescribed by the rehab team in Little Rock, she saw no problem. Everything was arranged, and within a few days after I was stable, I was transferred to HealthSouth in Fayetteville.

This was the smoothest transfer ever except for the nursing facility. I was greeted on a slow Sunday afternoon by a staff member who took charge from the minute Joshua stopped the car until I was admitted. He came to get me out of the car, with two medical assistants: one small older gentleman, and a tiny young lady.

I whispered to Joshua, "Please don't let them get me, they will drop me!" I had been dropped and mishandled so many times by now; I didn't look like I was heavy or hard to manage, but I was.

Joshua moved closer, but the tiny young lady said, "We have her, you go ahead and move your car and bring in her things and meet us in room 204."

Those two medical assistants worked like a well-oiled machine. They knew how to carefully transfer me from the car to the wheelchair and into the facility. By the time

Joshua came in with my bags, they were almost finished processing me into the facility. The nursing staff was waiting to take over, to do the medical part of inprocessing. I thought to myself, *This is the treatment I needed for the past three years.* I bowed my head and thanked God out loud right then for allowing me to be here.

The first thing I remember the nurse saying to me was that she was glad I was there, and that if anyone could get me back on my feet it was going to be this facility. I asked her if she had read my records, and she said they all had and were all ready for the challenge. She said that she was going to pray that Dr. Bo would take my case. I asked her why, and she said that he was a believer in Jesus Christ and would do everything he could to help me. So I also started to pray that Dr. Bo would take my case. By now my hope had shrunk so small; my faith remained strong, but my desire to continue the journey was weak.

The next morning Dr. Bo entered my room, telling me he was going to be caring for me while I was there. Dr. Bo knew his limitations, and assured me he would be relying on our limitless God for direction. He spoke my language and kept his word. He made sure I understood that all three of the teams (occupational, physical, and speech) had a job to do, and some days were going to be tough, but if I kept my faith, stayed motivated, and put forth my best effort, I would leave better than when I arrived.

The next months were extremely difficult. I ended up back at the hospital with another short exacerbation, then went straight back to HealthSouth afterwards. It was obvious to everyone that I was getting stronger, but with no way of knowing when another exacerbation would come, we couldn't ever fully relax. We were all desperate to find out how to stop them.

One of my nurses, whose name I sadly have forgotten, was studying to become a nurse practitioner and told me her class had just finished their study of neurological diseases. She said that there were a lot of cutting-edge therapies being put into trials, and she thought I should search the internet and apply to participate in a trial. Toward the end of her shift that evening she took me down to the resource center and we searched together. There were several trials being conducted in Canada, Mexico, and other countries, but limited trials here in the United States. We did find one being conducted in Chicago, and felt encouraged after reading about a recent patient's journey.

My nurse helped me with the questions and submitted the application to be admitted to the trial. I shrugged my shoulders, prayed, and thought to myself, *I don't have anything to lose*. Then I forgot about it until that nurse came to my section of the hospital a couple of weeks later. The first thing she asked me was whether I checked for a response email. I hadn't, because I didn't want to be disappointed.

To my surprise, when I did check my email, the trial team had reached out to me and wanted me to come to Chicago for evaluation. I needed to complete my current therapy; however, the team advised that the sooner the evaluation, the better the outcome.

The first step was to get strong enough to get to Chicago. It was a challenge for me even to hold my body up, but every day I felt stronger and stronger, and soon I was able to travel with help on a private medical flight provided by an organization called Mercy Angels.

Dr. Burt, who was in charge of the trial, explained the entire process, from the pre-trial through post-trial procedures. The constant during the conversation was how sick the transplant was going to make me before I would start to feel better.

The bottom line for me was that I met the criteria to be considered for the trial, but I was too weak to get started. Dr. Burt explained that the trial would involve hematopoietic stem cell transplantation (HCST), which would cause me to be so ill that I might die. Stem cell transplantation is a specific form of a bone marrow transplant, so my bone marrow would be replaced with bone marrow clear of neuromyelitis optica.

We are all born with bone marrow. After some time, bone marrow is usually only found in the hips and torso. Bone marrow contains stem cells, which are referred to as pluripotent, meaning that they can become other cells in the body. So the first step in the transplant would be to stimulate my stem cells to "overgrow" and extract some of my bone marrow so those stem cells could be harvested from it.

Next, my cells that were carrying the disease would be destroyed with chemotherapy, which is very dangerous. I would be vulnerable to any infection because I would have no white blood cells to fight off pathogens.

Finally, the stem cells would be transplanted back into my bone marrow, where they would begin to crowd out any remaining diseased cells that had been causing my body to attack itself.

The chemotherapy treatments, in addition to the transplant, can be too much to handle, so the decision to go forward was difficult. And after enduring all of that, there was a possibility that the process wouldn't work. The best possible outcome would require me to start out strong and as healthy as possible. He told us that I probably needed a couple of months to be strong enough to begin.

I finished my current physical therapy program and was discharged from the facility to start the home therapy program. I was glad to be home, but I wasn't able to do very much. My body was still weak, and I was still in the wheelchair, unable to walk. Home therapy went well, and I learned to vacuum, load the dishwasher, and wash and fold clothes from the wheelchair. I gained strength and continued to focus on the trial.

The main issue at this point was the financial side. I knew insurance wouldn't cover any part of the transplant because it was in the trial stage, and they had already denied everything else, so we still had to come up with $30,000 before we could be scheduled to move forward. I remember asking the financial advisor where people came up with $30,000 after exhausting their savings, retirement, and everything else they could to stay alive. She said, "They just find a way."

I asked for prayer from different organizations I was a part of, and we did find a way. Some people who donated funds remembered me singing and praying bedside with their family as their loved one transitioned out of this life. I've sung all over NWA and beyond, mostly for free, and I always felt that these were divine opportunities. I don't even know all the people who gave so I could get a transplant. I do know that many of them were from the VA Medical Center in Fayetteville, Arkansas; the Christian Women's Club in Bentonville, Arkansas; FBC Bentonville; FBC Bentonville Women's Department; FBC Choir; and East Mount Olive Baptist Church in Port Arthur, Texas. I am grateful to everyone who gave, and sent personal thank-you notes to everyone I had email or mailing addresses for. I used those notes as hand therapy to develop the tiny tendons and muscles necessary for writing and typing.

It wasn't long before we were ready to move forward. I had a return appointment with Dr. Burt, who accepted me for the trial. He told us he would begin testing in one month, and said the only thing he needed was for my primary care provider (PCP) and current neurologist to agree to my continuing on to the trial. I came home to prepare to be away from home until the transplant was complete.

I took the procedure paperwork to my PCP, Dr. Byrum, to review. He thought the transplant was too risky. I had an appointment the following week in Little Rock with my current neurologist, who also advised against participating in the trial. He felt that the transplant needed to be approved by the FDA before we pursued it. He told me I should be thankful that I was alive, and that this transplant could kill me.

I had been told that my life was going to be short anyway because of the NMO disease process and the constant severity of my exacerbations. The problem with waiting for FDA approval was that the disease is rare, and it is difficult even to be considered for the transplant trial, but the FDA can only approve a procedure after enough positive data is received.

I was very disappointed with what my PCP and neurologist were saying, and made up my mind that I had nothing to lose. I was going to die whether I had the transplant or not. At least this way I'd be a part of the data to help others. Just before I needed to leave for Chicago to do the pre-trial testing, I met with Dr. Byrum again. He told me that after speaking with Dr. Burt and giving it some thought, he had had a change of heart, and thought it would be all right to go forward with the transplant. That was one of the happiest days in a long time.

We finally had everything in place, the appointment was set, and my sister Sherida flew with me to Chicago as my transplant nurse. All the testing took about two weeks: lab work, MRIs, pulmonary testing, and ophthalmology, just to name a few.

The first step of the actual hematopoietic stem cell transplant was to overgrow my stem cells. This was done with injections every day, pushing my body to produce more cells. The next step was to harvest the cells from my bone marrow. Once harvested, the stem cells were processed in the lab to make sure they were free of disease. The cells were then stored, waiting for transplant back into my body after chemotherapy. The intention was to stop my body from attacking itself, which would, theoretically, stop the exacerbations.

I was very ill after the transplant. The chemotherapy had left my immune system very weak, and we were in Chicago for seven weeks until Dr. Burt felt the transplant was a success and I could safely travel back home to finish recovering.

I will not regain what I lost, since spinal cord damage (for now) is permanent. I haven't lost any more strength or function since the transplant. As with all medical discoveries, every patient responds differently, and what worked for me may not work for the next patient. I am so grateful that my data is now being used to make a determination as to whether HSCT can be used as a treatment for others diagnosed with neuromyelitis optica. My living through this trial is not in vain.

In all respects, the transplant was considered a success. I have had no other exacerbations since the transplant, and continue to be well.

BIG SISTER

My Sister Sherida's Witness

Growing up, I took a lot of flak for my sister Timesia. Mother would say, "Why did you allow that to happen, Sherida? You are the oldest."

Five years' difference in age never made a difference in our relationship; we are as close as if there were no years separating us. Having each other made certain that we would always have at least one friend. Timi was always bigger than all of us, so people assumed she was the oldest. Plus, there was never a shy bone in her body, which made it normal for her to take charge.

We are all so much like our Mother: seeing good in people and overlooking the bad, always trying to do anything we can to help someone out, and giving our last if it is going to put a smile on another's face. My lil' sister and best friend has been the glue in our family, so having to step up while she was sick meant putting on some big shoes, but I knew it had to be done.

We'd faced challenges like any other family, so when

we met in the hospital that Friday night not even knowing what was going on, we showed up to do what we have always done: get this over and done with.

As time went on, like everyone else I wondered, "Where in the world are you, God?" My coping language is laughter. "The joy of the Lord is my strength," and during the most difficult times I can remember finding anything I could to laugh about, and oh my goodness, so much of my laughter turned right into tears.

One of the most difficult points was the day they were going to intubate my sister because her lungs were not functioning properly. The doctors informed us that they weren't sure if she would make it. We had prayed about it and had no doubt that everything was going to be okay, but it took everything we had to hold on. Losing my sister was not an option. She had been through every treatment available, but she was steadily getting worse. We needed a miracle.

After wheeling Timi into the ICU, a nurse directed Mother and me to the waiting room and said they would come for us when Timesia was stable. We were exhausted, and I think we fell asleep. My eyes opened to see a strange-looking gentleman standing over Mother and me. He began encouraging us with the same scriptures that we had been praying over, as if he had been with us the past few weeks. I was focused on his bow-tie that looked like a butterfly waving at me, while Mother wondered how his silver hair was blowing without a breeze in the room.

When we could go back and see Timi, the first thing we told her about was the gentleman who appeared to us out of nowhere.

She said, "Wait a minute, did he have on a checkered blazer?"

Mother and I couldn't remember the jacket, but we told her about his hair and the bow-tie. No matter what he had worn, we knew for certain he had spoken encouragement to us through scripture that we had prayed over many times. No one else saw the man but the three of us. We concluded that God had given us a sign to continue trusting Him; that He was still with us and we were going to make it through with the help of this gentleman angel.

Our road from that point on wasn't easy, but God kept His promises. He was with us every step of the way. I had gone to the altar at my church Sunday after Sunday to pray over my sister and my family. One Sunday when I was in the prayer line again, the Minister spoke to me and said that God had heard every single prayer concerning my sister, and was waiting for our praise. Armed with this information, I ran to my car to call Timesia and tell her to begin singing (which is her love language) to God.

She was so upset with me—she said, "I cannot even breathe, let alone sing. What is wrong with you, Sherida?"

What had seemed so profound to me, Timi didn't get right away; but I went ahead and started praising instead of praying. Somewhere along the way, everyone in our family, including Timesia, did the same thing. It was an amazing blessing to see God at work acknowledging our praise.

My encouragement to those reading these words is, "Never let go of God." Trust His word. He has a purpose and a plan for everything He allows us to go through. Accept your trials, learn from them, and then turn around and use them to bless others. This is my sister's calling.

One week later, on a Sunday afternoon, we got a call from Timi's voice-activated phone, but it automatically hung up after a few minutes of silence. I think it was because she had to do recovery breathing after each song, but she wanted us to know she was singing.

A week later, we were told that Timi would be going through a series of psychological tests. There were so many physical issues warranting Timesia's declining mental state that we hadn't entertained any of those concerns yet! After speaking to Timi, we all had a better view of what was really going on.

Several nurses had reported a "loud outburst of singing" progressing into an "unexplained bout of laughter" several times that week, and thought an evaluation was necessary. They noted coming into the room one time because her singing was at the top of her lungs, and she seemed "out of it." But we all knew that Timi had made it back to her norm, and that after the evaluation, they too would understand that this was her coping mechanism rather than a mental breakdown.

* * *

Sherida is the sweetest person you could ever meet. I've taken notes from her all my life, and aspire to have her tender heart and be as soft-spoken and generous as she is. She has always been vertically challenged, so she was never a match for me physically except for one time, which I'll tell you about shortly. Sherida is humble and meek, and has always been there for me. I couldn't have made it without her love and support as she carried my entire family through this journey.

Growing up, I made things difficult for Rida. I was always into something, and when I'd get into trouble, she knew what was coming, but she never complained about it. She assumed the responsibilities of the oldest, and all that went with that.

I will never forget the day she decided to move out of our house and stay with her best friend. I just didn't know how I would live without my sister. We remained close until I went into the military. After I finished my service obligation, we picked right back up as if I'd never left. Our relationship is rare: we live and love through the good, bad, and ugly. I will never even come close to being to her what she has been to me and my family, but I'll never tire of trying.

Everyone was working, including Rida, when we found out I'd been accepted for the transplant, but it was a no-brainer who would be accompanying me. The only one it could be was Sherida Thrift.

The trip to Chicago for preliminary testing had a few issues. We went through all of the classes and got acquainted with the area, but there was nothing to prepare us for negative-23-degree weather. We made several trips back to Chicago to get pre-transplant medication, to learn to give the injections to over-grow my cells, and finally for the transplant.

The final trip Rida and I made together was the worst one. I had gotten into trouble with her on the previous trip. Things hadn't turned out too well for me the night I decided I could take myself to the bathroom, when I woke up on the floor to her telling me that she was in charge, and that I better not dare breathe without her approval. You'd think that would have been enough to make me want to follow her directions to a tee.

For the most part I did follow her directions. But after being in Chicago together for eight weeks, you can imagine we were really starting to bump heads a little. Toward the end, I started feeling a little better one moment, and then horrible the next, which was as expected. I wasn't able to do much, but no one could tell me otherwise.

We'd collected too much stuff during the eight weeks we were there, and had a strict weight limit due to the tiny medical aircraft we'd be coming back on. Rida had already planned to take some things to the post office to mail out, but I wanted to go with her to give her a hand. She told me she could go much faster if she left me, not to mention that I needed to rest for the trip the next day, but I kept pushing, and then it happened: the one time she was a match for me. She opened up on me and let me have it. I'd never seen her that way, and am okay if I never see that side of her ever again.

It wasn't long before I realized I didn't have a choice but to do exactly what that four-foot nine-inch lady told me to do, and keep my mouth closed until we made it home. I was actually scared—after all, I was really at her mercy. I thought she'd never get it all out of her system. Every time there was a pause, she'd think about something else I'd done during this time and start fussing about that.

I was so happy to get on that private plane, put on those headphones, and not hear her fussing at me any more. I knew it was bad when she called Mother and said she was going to leave me in Chicago. I closed my mouth and didn't open it again until she told me to. After all she went through to help me despite my own stubbornness, I guess I deserved all that fussing.

Sherida was great at giving directions to Joshua, the girls, Kitty, and Mother, making things easier for us after the transplant. They rotated through to take over my care while Rida went back home to Dallas.

Every family needs a Sherida, the faithful thread that quietly intertwines throughout the family, mending brokenness. She knows her calling and doesn't get confused about it. Her character lines up with the word of God, and she is a bright light shining for Jesus. As we've shared memories from this experience, I've learned to appreciate her even more for how she took care of me while working through everything else going on in our family. Sherida led our family in growing through this journey.

I KNEW MY WIFE
WOULD WALK AGAIN

My Husband Joshua's Witness

From the very beginning, I felt like my wife would walk again. I just didn't know how.

One morning we were getting ready for what we thought was a normal Monday. Then Timesia came into the living room saying that her legs felt very heavy and tight. Before she could finish what she was saying, she fell hard to the floor. I helped her up, and she fell again several times. We looked at each other and shrugged, because we didn't know what to make of this. I told her I'd take Dee to school because she needed to make a doctor's appointment to see what was going on.

I was happily surprised to see her home when I got home from work, until she stood up and started to walk. It was like she was inebriated. We just attributed it to her overdoing everything the previous week. She had traveled for her birthday, and didn't get enough rest.

Things got worse over the next few days. By Thursday,

her doctor said she needed to go to the ER. After numerous tests, it was decided that she should be transported to UAMS in Little Rock. The weakness was from her waist down, and she could no longer walk.

I felt helpless as I watched Timesia being loaded into the ambulance stretcher from the hospital bed. I didn't know what I was going to do. I went to pick Dee up, and everything felt so strange. After getting dinner, and getting Diana ready for bed and for school the next day, I went down to my study and prayed over the situation. I felt the weight of the world on my shoulders.

The person impacted the worst was Diana. Very early in the morning I had to get her up and take her to someone in our great support network who would get her ready for school, since I had to be to work early. She did better some days than others.

She went to an after-school program, and I would pick her up after work. The new routine was difficult for Diana because she was used to after-school activities, both at school and church, and she took piano lessons every other day. I started to realize that I wouldn't be able to keep any of it up, so I told Diana that things would be different for some time until we could get back to normal.

The Bible speaks of the man leading his family as Jesus leads His church, and I knew that's what I had to do. I'd say to God, "You know what is best, and you don't put more on us than we can bear," but I felt God was giving me too much credit.

Every weekend we went to see Timi. Once I was off work on Fridays I would pick up Dee, grab a bite, and head to Little Rock. There was a time that it got to me. When we arrived, Timi wanted to talk about the insurance policy, and said we should just leave and not come back—that we should forget about her to die there. In all the time we had been going through this, that was the first time I cried once we were back home. Of course, we kept on going to see her until we were able to bring her home.

This was the biggest challenge I had faced in my life. I knew she would recover, and walk again, but I didn't know how. I was encouraged when I had a dream where I saw Timi walking. I prayed for patience, because it was getting to the point that I was losing it. I prayed one night: "God, you know how much Timi loves to sing praises to You, would You give her a chance to do that."

I knew everything would be all right if she could just get to that point. The first time she was able to sing again in church will be in my mind forever. I was out of my mind praising God as she was singing to the Lord.

My advice to anyone who finds themselves in this kind of a battle is to be sure to pray and read scripture over the situation. Having a good support system is vital, especially with small children. Remain patient, and trust God; He won't let you down. Be careful not to give up before God gives up.

* * *

After the second major exacerbation, once I was on a treatment plan at the University of Arkansas Medical Center (UAMS), I always looked forward to the weekends. I knew I would be able to eat, because Joshua and Dee would be there to feed me, and I would be able to have a good shower. Joshua had been with me through my previous major neck, back, and rotator cuff surgeries and recoveries, so this was somewhat familiar territory for him.

The best thing was when J and Dee would take me out of the hospital. As soon as we would get outside, they would stand on either side of me and help me stand up. I would be propped up on them, but that didn't matter; it was great. I had learned a lot about therapy, and one thing I knew was that supported standing would remind my brain what to do and help my nerves and muscles fire up.

Sometimes Joshua and Dee would get to the hospital during my therapy. I didn't like that at all, because I wasn't able to do very much after the last exacerbation. The discouragement on Joshua's face made me so sad, because I was trying so hard. But Joshua and Dee would both follow the therapist's lead, cheering me on to keep on trying, and that inspired me to keep working hard.

One day we had talked through the necessities of the upcoming week, and I longed to know what Joshua was thinking about our situation. When I asked, he said that he wasn't thinking about any particulars, just going through the motions to survive. I really wanted to know how he was able to come back week after week, with me showing no signs of improvement. Joshua has always been a man of few words, and just the fact that he responded relieved me, but he never really answered my question.

During another visit, I asked him to come sit next to me on the bed (after three months in various care facilities, this was the longest time we'd ever been apart) and he asked me, "What would that do?" He was frustrated, and I interpreted that to mean he wanted me well and home. I felt so guilty for having this disease, and what it was doing to us, but there was nothing I could do about it.

Ater greeting me, he would sit in the chair for hours, with his hands interlocked, either praying, watching TV, or sleeping. I already felt like a monster, because even though my extremities looked normal, they felt like large uncontrollable objects attached to me. In my mind, my husband no longer saw me as attractive or desirable, which is an agony I am unable to describe.

When he looked at me while we talked, the pity in his eyes made me so sad, I'd fight back the tears until they would leave and I could cry myself to sleep. However, in a way this only motivated me to push harder. I did all the work I was advised to do because I wanted to be "normal again" and just go back home with my husband and family.

By this time I'd lost a lot of weight, mostly muscle, which is of course vital for holding the body up. I couldn't even feed myself. There was always an enormous patient load on the stroke/spinal cord injury section of the hospital, making it difficult for the nurses to feed everyone. I had sores in my mouth from the medication, so there were many things I couldn't eat.

Joshua did some research and came up with a smoothie recipe that turned my ability to eat completely around. It was packed with vital nutrients: protein, probiotics, fruits and veggies. He made it fresh every morning, and continues to make it today—we even have most of our family drinking it. I was unable to feed myself for a long time, and he fed me without hesitation. I could lower my head and drink this smoothie, and not worry about whether I would have anything else to eat.

As you already know, the hospital gave up on me and called Joshua to come and take me to the nursing facility. That was one of our saddest, darkest days. When he arrived at the hospital that morning, he was physically upset, which I'd never seen. He seemed angry at the world. He wanted me to be able to do more, and thought the medical team hadn't given me enough time and had just given up on me when my recovery didn't fit their quotas.

Joshua didn't sign up for any of what was happening to me, but he walked through it like a champ. We were told early on that marriages don't usually survive what we were going through. When I heard that, I made a mental note reminding myself that God said we should remain together until death parted us. I have wondered to myself, *Why did Joshua stay with me during this journey?* It would have made more sense for him to pull away while I was down, but he didn't. In fact, he was as all in like never before. But then, he has always gone about things differently.

I prayed that God would physically restore me to be able to come home and take care of Joshua and Diana. I was extremely motivated, and I never accepted "disability," but looked at it as the ability to do things differently. My life lens focused on being my best for them, to come through this long battle with victory, while walking in the will of God. I wanted to be the wife and mother I once was; my family deserved that. Joshua was a huge part of why I fought so hard.

Somewhere along the way, there was a disconnect, and way too much distance between us. Going through such difficulty, the depth of one's love is obvious. I think when a person hasn't been exposed to genuine love, it is hard for them to recognize, and can even make them afraid. This is what I've told myself in consolation for Joshua's pulling away not long after I got back on my feet.

He had put everything on hold, and once we could do more than just focus on my survival, I think he just wanted to go back to normal. But NMO was a part of me now, and I needed to start giving back in gratitude for my second lease on life. I'm still grateful that Joshua did the best he knew how to handle all he was faced with. He took excellent care of Diana, and has always provided for us.

Joshua eventually had a hard time believing all of this could happen to one person, and accused me of making it up and being selfish and inconsiderate. He would get upset about help from others and wanted to know why I was asking so many people for help. I told him that I didn't ask, they just volunteered. I realize now that he didn't understand that this was their love language.

Everywhere I looked I saw couples going through their trial together, shouldering each other through. I wanted that, and for the hardest times it was that way, but the day came that the burden was too much, and his support was gone without warning. For some time I pretended and made excuses, hoping that things would get better. For years I was just thankful that we made it and were still standing, able to tell the story. That was huge for me, but it wasn't enough for both of us.

My entire family has suffered with me through this battle. I have numerous medical issues, but far less than before the transplant, and I am thankful for the outcome I have. My physical appearance is not as it was twenty years ago. I have constant physical and mental fatigue. I have PTSD, anxiety, and stress over many things, but what my family has had to endure because of me is the one thing that keeps me awake at night. I recognize the enormous load everyone had to carry.

It is human nature when you are suffering to want connection from your loved ones. I know that I was needy, but there was no way around it. I was dependent because I was unable to do anything for myself—a humbling experience for an independent person like me. I was already beating myself up because I wasn't able to take care of my family.

My take-away is that there is really no way to know what triggers another human being. You can think you know someone very well, and end up finding out you don't know them at all. Going through a traumatic experience brings out who we really are, and I tend to expect to receive what I give, but I am often disappointed. I expected that when I was better, our relationship would also be stronger. But that's not the way it turned out, and I am finally accepting that it is impossible to make another person love you, whether in sickness or in health.

This part of my story has been difficult for me to write, but I am sharing it to encourage you, whether you are in a fight for your life surrounded by a loving family, finding yourself in the trenches alone, or some of both:

First, never accept the guilt for having a disease.

Next, keep your head up. When fear creeps in and you look around and there is no one standing with you, find the courage tucked deep inside, and stand until you can take a step.

Finally, encourage yourself to focus and take one step at a time. You are never truly alone.

I have found freedom in releasing what I am not able to control. Today I offer you the opportunity to be free of what is holding you captive. The most beautiful gift isn't always wrapped in a perfect package; it might be where you least expect it. God has His own way of giving, and we may miss out if we are looking for glitter and bling. My blessing in disguise during this process has been a closer connection with Him and with my own sense of purpose.

AFTER TRANSPLANT

2015

After getting through the initial recovery period, I endured another course of physical, speech, and occupational therapy in order to get back to a normal lifestyle—not my normal, but a new normal. We didn't know what I'd be able to do once everything was settled, so we started with the very basics. Each therapist took their expertise seriously in order to get all my disconnected body functions working again.

My body was my exercise equipment for a long time. Learning to sit up straight in the wheelchair until I was able to stand was my workout for weeks. Bringing a spoon, my toothbrush, or a cup up to my mouth were all difficult tasks that I did over and over again before becoming proficient. I then graduated to dressing myself, transferring from my wheelchair to the sofa, and so forth until I reached a good level of function.

One day I was feeling very confident and just wanted to do the things I enjoyed doing for my family, like cooking.

I decided to make a pot of beans. I washed, soaked, and seasoned the beans so they were all ready to be cooked. I rested after my therapy session, as I always did. Then I got started with cooking the beans.

I was still struggling with a lot of uncontrolled spasms in my lower extremities. As I stood propped against my wheelchair working on those beans, a spasm started in the upper part of my thigh and soon became so severe I knew I should sit. But when I tried to sit, I missed the chair, and on my way down my head hit the corner of the bar, resulting in my getting fifteen staples. Nevertheless, we enjoyed our beans that night for dinner.

Exercising has been a part of my life since the military, but I started losing muscle mass when the severity of the pain made exercise difficult, and of course lost even more when I was paralyzed. So I used my smarts to create an exercise program using my housework. Cooking, cleaning, laundry, and taking care of the lawn are all a part of the program. I take pride in being a good steward over my blessings. My family remains one of my greatest joys, and in my heart I've given one hundred percent. I have tried to create a clean, safe environment for talking, sharing, laughing, and even some quiet time.

Walking remains a daily task I deliberately work at improving. I've learned to conserve my energy to be able to accomplish what I need to in a given day, something I didn't even think about before I went down with NMO. Because of the brain damage I experienced, I spend as much time exercising mentally as I do physically. I have to concentrate on what I want to communicate and have the conversation with myself long before having it with someone else, and I still have a difficult time. There are so many things I wish were better, but the good continues to outweigh the bad.

My life today is completely dependent on God, which is the way He wants it to be all the time, not just when we have a problem. God has my undivided attention, which took my relationship with Him to a different level. I've learned that He wants all of me, not just my leftovers. I am always stronger coming through a trial. God receives all the glory and honor as my faith is increased.

I was raised to know that giving up is never an option, and all three of my daughters have been raised the same. I am not a "woe is me" kind of person—I try really hard to see what I can gain from a bad situation. Sometimes that is hard to know; however, when the time is right, there is clarity.

Looking in my rear-view mirror, I can see so many mistakes I made; however, my deliberate approach, then and now, is how I persevered. I don't lay down my weapons until there is nothing left to fight. My positive attitude is one of the weapons in my arsenal, fueled by the promises of God.

GIVING THANKS

My Mother's Witness, Continued

The next time I saw Timi was Thanksgiving. She and her family hosted us before the transplant, and we've been rejoicing since. Her incredible story magnifies the power of God.

There is no explanation for my daughter's recovery (according to the chief of neurology at UAMS), except by the grace of God. The transplant helped her, but the FDA has not approved the transplant as treatment because there are others who have had the same transplant and saw no change. The chemo and plasmapheresis before that actually made her worse, in my opinion.

I recently retired from my lifelong experience working in the hospital, but watching my daughter's health battle strengthened me the most for what I do today. Since retiring, I am now my husband's caretaker. He has Alzheimer's and dementia, neurological conditions that have mentally incapacitated him. Looking at him, you would never know, but hang with him a few and you realize something isn't right.

We never would have imagined that John would be in the condition he is today, but the same goes for Timesia. She was the one in our family who, after serving in the United States Army, helped us change some of our eating habits. She has always been spiritually strong. When I am down, I can always call Timesia. She has a way of lifting me up and getting me back on track.

Timesia has always been the one who simply deals with whatever happens. In this case she had no choice; this disease hit head-on without a warning. It completely took over her body. NMO nearly destroyed my daughter physically, mentally, and even spiritually.

I'll never forget her asking me, "Mother, how in the world can I glorify God with this mangled-up body?" which I couldn't answer.

What I know now is that God was and is being glorified every day of her life. From the time she gets up in the morning until she finally lies down at night, she is at work bringing glory to God.

I am confident that the love in our family for each other and for Jesus was our major defense. We are not a perfect family. Through the course of this battle we have had arguments, been upset with one another, and fill in the blanks—we went through all of it. One time while Rida and Timi were in Chicago, Rida called me because she was so angry with Timesia (and Rida never gets mad unless pushed to the extreme).

She said, "Mother, I've had it with your daughter. I'm about to walk out and leave her in this place."

In the background, I could hear Timi's faint voice: "Mother help me, help me Mother."

I couldn't figure out what pushed Rida to that point. Then I thought, *She has been in Chicago for weeks now with Timesia, the world's worst patient.* I talked her down off the ledge and they got on that tiny medical aircraft to go home. Timi said Rida stayed upset all the way home, and wouldn't talk to her, so she put on the headset and talked to the pilot. I freely share this story because even the best stories, if the truth be told, have some bad parts to them. It is what you do with the bad that impacts the outcome.

We are better for going through this, but it was not a walk-in-the-park experience. I am thankful for the small role I played, but the champion is Timesia. She has shown us all how to take life as it comes, and no matter the difficulty, how to make it a point to have the very best response.

This book has been a long time coming, but there aren't enough words, time, or energy to describe what we went through. My prayer is that after reading this book, you are encouraged, but most of all, that you prepare yourself. We never know what is going to happen to us in life. You can have it all together, and then out of nowhere be hit with a rare disease or some other battle you never saw coming.

Timesia's purpose in life is far from over, and I am excited for all there is to come.

DOCTOR'S SUMMARY

Dr. Byrum, Primary Care Provider

A s of this summary, Timesia is alive and active, seven years out from her stem cell transplant. She has a weak gait and trips and falls at times, but she is able to walk up and down steps unassisted. She does not use a wheelchair, walker, or cane. She has no observable weakness in her upper extremities. Her foot drop is resolved. She recently completed a Livestrong rehabilitation physical therapy program where she was involved in an aggressive strengthening program. She has a good quality of life. She has not had an NMO exacerbation since her stem cell transplant, and has not received IV steroids or Rituxan since then either.

In summary, Timesia has a history of neuromyelitis optica, initially presenting as right optic neuritis and a left thalamic lesion, which resolved with steroid treatment. Three years later, she was diagnosed with NMO after seeing multiple specialists. She was treated with IV steroids, Rituxan, and plasmapheresis, all of which yielded some benefit. However, recurrent severe exacerbations with varying levels of weakness, numbness, spasms, foot drop, and cranial nerve palsy eventually progressed to severe disability, abnormal spinal MRI findings and myelomalacia, prompting her to seek stem cell transplantation ten years after her initial NMO symptoms. Since her transplant, her NMO appears quiescent, and it appears that her only residual symptoms relate to damage to her spinal cord from her prior NMO exacerbations. In light of the fact that she is no longer receiving specific treatment for NMO, her clinical course suggests that she is cured.

Jim Byrum MD
Internal Medicine and Pediatrics

WHAT COMES NEXT?

This journey has redefined my life on so many levels. For so long I've had the fairy tale mentality: "and they lived happily ever after." To date, my experience is definitely not the ending I had in mind. My prayer is to encourage you not to ever give up, even when things don't go the way you think they should.

Every painful memory shared here encourages me. While only God knows why this has been my course, as long as He is glorified, it is all good — in fact, I have a song called "It's All Good." This unpredictable course keeps going, and I don't have a clue what comes next, but God does.

God gave me music that I've had to sing alone to myself. My prayers became so sincere; I mean, I had nothing but time to pray. I found myself praying with others while in private agony weighing me down to despair. I had so much pride and didn't want to be the milk carton lady who always has some problem, so I pretended I was okay, and suffered quietly through defeat. I talked myself into believing that things weren't so bad. I felt like I was letting God down while I was down in this valley. I had to learn to take a dose of everything I had been pouring into others.

Looking in my rear-view mirror revealed that I've been here before, in different circumstances; not as extreme, but similar experiences throughout my life. God used those seasons as stepping stones to take me higher. Nothing is lost to God: the hurt, fear, burdens, and being misused during this season will all work to make me a better servant. After every public speaking event, I hear, "It is hard to believe what you said; you don't look like what you've been through." That's because God is the keeper of my soul. My flesh has been crushed at times, but my spirit remains strong.

I can say that God is the keeper of my soul, because I have been in distress and had Him rescue me. My testimony of knowing God comes through being given up on by doctors more than once, and then being restored by Him. The only way to know the Comforter is to survive the mental anguish of loss or a physical crisis.

I learned the power of prayer, and found myself praying for perfect strangers and their families. Seeing God's faithfulness was so encouraging to me and to those God placed in my path. It was prayer that helped me focus on something other than my situation, and that is when things started turning around for me.

Moving forward, I am certain God will continue what He has begun in me. I continue to surrender to His will for what comes next. I have a hard time when I do not feel in control (I bet you can relate), but the truth is that I've never been in control. I have made a conscious, deliberate choice to depend on Him, and He desires that from all of us. This is not an easy path for me, but I know it is the right thing to do.

I never say that I am disabled; rather, I say I have the ability to do things differently. I have learned to take my mind (as difficult as neurological damage sometimes makes it to put thoughts together), my body (with its loss of vision, tricky balance, shortness of breath, decreased sensation, and weakness), and my soul (humbled but unbroken), and present them to the Lord, that He would use all of me for His glory.

I thought fighting to live would be the last battle I'd face. I thought I'd tell my hard little story, and end with "but we all made it out just fine." But that's not the case. Since we are all still human, we keep facing struggles.

I do have an idea that this will work out all right, because I have read "the end of the book" in the gospel. I know that this story has to work for my good, because it brings glory to God. I am fortunate, because I know what God says about me, and this frees me to live an abundant life until I die, without guilt or apology.

LIVING TO WIN FOUNDATION

There are advancements being made for many well-known neurological diseases, such as Multiple Sclerosis (MS), Parkinson's, and Alzheimer's, to name a few. NMO was reported for many years as a variant of MS, but the National Institutes of Health (NIH) now recognizes NMO as a separate, rare disease, reporting up to 15,000 cases in the United States, and 1-2 cases per 100,000 people worldwide. Of those cases, the prognosis is poor for many, partly due to the difficulty of proper diagnosis.

I founded the Living to Win (L2W) Foundation, a 501c3 nonprofit, in October 2017, to support patients and their families, helping them stay motivated to fight and survive neuromyelitis optica. This was a direct response to my own struggles through misdiagnosis, treatment, and rehabilitation, as well as the conflict with insurance.

My arduous journey made crystal clear the necessity for such a foundation. After literally getting my feet back on the ground, I knew I had to do everything I could to raise awareness about the disease. I felt then, and still feel today, an urgent obligation to educate the medical community, including doctors, other health care professionals, insurance companies, and government elected officials; as well as patients and their family members, who are usually called upon to be caretakers. In 2017, we prayed and felt that the Lord led us to the right people who would take on the commitment of helping us help others, and the L2W Board of Directors were sworn in. We are thankful that four of the original directors and some wonderful new faces and voices are still advancing the Foundation's mission today.

The primary goal after starting the foundation was the massive mission of advocating on every level. I would not be able to offer much if I hadn't gone through this myself. I trusted both my primary care physicians (mine at the VAMC and our family physician) because they always took the time to listen, which is rare. Working for a primary care physician as a medical coordinator taught me exactly how a medical encounter should be handled, from the patient's medical history to the very end of the appointment. My extensive training while working for a physician allowed me to learn a vast amount about the medical profession that I wouldn't have otherwise known. I do not think this was a coincidence.

That knowledge paid off when I began my journey with NMO. I knew I was limited, but I was also armed with tools to fight for myself, which is one of the reasons I made it through. I remember talking to both doctors about the first unusual, subtle, but very painful symptom that surfaced. Their response was almost identical, both taking their own approach but getting to the bottom of what I was experiencing. My medical history complicated things for some time, but they both kept at it until they ran out of answers before consulting with a neurologist.

Each doctor tried to fit my symptoms into a box: their goal was to obtain a diagnosis. It was very frustrating when they decided it was one thing, and then discovered it wasn't. I can remember saying to each of them at one time or another, "We have done MRI's, and I have taken the medications as you have prescribed. I am not out of my mind, nor am I making things up. There is something more going on," and the digging would start over again.

There were no NMO support groups—in fact, the limited information available when I was properly diagnosed was from the Guthy-Jackson Foundation (whose mission is research for a cure for NMO), and the Mayo Clinic. I consulted with a neurologist at the Mayo Clinic, but they didn't have an opportunity for me to go there because I was too sick. They did ask for my blood work to use for their research, which we agreed to.

My situation was very difficult: diagnosed with a rare disease, having limited resources and no support. Looking back, God was directing me to keep fighting for myself then, as He is directing me to fight for others today.

God's direction has positioned Living to Win to speak with neurological teams, using my experience to help them see things from the patient's view. We've had opportunities to bring awareness to the community through various events. We have come alongside patients and their families to offer support while they are navigating their way through the often lonesome, dark, and scary pathway to health and recovery from NMO.

Moving forward, we look with great anticipation for opportunities to speak with insurance companies and our local, state, and national elected officials, to discuss approving cutting-edge discoveries sooner as possible treatments, as well as insurance covering claims for these treatments. This would be a gigantic step in a positive direction, in which the patient would benefit from focusing on their health rather than concerning themselves with financial burdens or having to battle just to get access to a new treatment that might help them.

L2W operates on a limited budget of donations from two major events each year. We hold Biking to Win (B2W), a family-friendly event with riders donating in order to participate. This event is also to help show that our bodies are stronger than we think they are: after being paralyzed for eight months, I can ride twenty miles by the grace of God.

Our other annual event is Worship to Win (W2W), a gospel concert with many talented musicians. While this is a fundraising event, it is also another way to give glory to God for all He has done, and our way to offer inspiration and give back to our supporters. Every vital organ was injured while I was down, including my lungs. I don't command the smooth voice or the range I used to, but I am blessed to be able to perform in our concert and glad to use every bit of what I have to minister to the needs of others.

We have applied for several grants from various pharmaceutical companies that manufacture the medications used to treat the symptoms of NMO, as well as grants from medical service organizations.

L2W is limited in how much we can assist patients with NMO. It would be a blessing to have the resources available to meet as many of their massive physical, spiritual, and mental needs as possible. We always hope and pray for resources and opportunities to manifest.

www.LivingToWin.org

HEALING SCRIPTURES

What I Believe

Jesus is the Lord of my life. Sickness and disease have no power over me. I am forgiven and am free from sin and guilt. I am dead to sin, and alive to righteousness. *See Colossians 1:21-22.*

No evil will befall me, neither shall any plague come near my dwelling. For You have given Your angels charge over me. They keep my pathway, which is life, healing, and health. *See Psalms 91:10-11 and Proverbs 12:28.*

Jesus took my infirmities and bore my sickness. Therefore, I refuse to allow sickness to dominate my body. The life of God flows within me, bringing healing to every fiber of my being. *See Matthew 8:17 and John 6:63.*

I command my blood cells to destroy every disease, germ, and virus that tries to inhabit my body. I command every cell of my body to restore life and health abundantly. *See Proverbs 12:14 and 14:30.*

Scriptures

"O Lord my God, I cried unto Thee, and Thou hast healed me." –Psalm 30:2

"… but they that seek the Lord shall not want any good thing." –Psalm 34:10b

"Many are the afflictions of the righteous: but the Lord delivered him out of them all." –Psalm 34:19

"He hath delivered my soul in peace from the battle that was against me: for there were many with me." –Psalm 55:18

"Have mercy on me, O lord, for I am weak; O Lord, heal me, for my bones are troubled." –Psalm 6:2

" … He preserveth the souls of His saints, He delivereth them out of the hand of the wicked." –Psalm 97:10b

"Who forgiveth all thine iniquities; Who healeth all thy diseases." –Psalm 103:3

"I will never forget Thy precepts for with them Thou has quickened me." –Psalm 119:93

"Surely, He hath borne our griefs, and carried our sorrows ..." –Isaiah 53:4a

"But He was wounded for our transgressions, He was bruised for our iniquities: the chastisement of our peace was upon Him; and by His stripes we are healed." –Isaiah 53:5

"If the Son therefore shall make you free, ye shall be free indeed." –John 8:36

"For the law of the Spirit of life in Christ Jesus hath made me free from the law of sin and death." –Romans 8:2

"He that spared not His own Son, but delivered Him up for us all, how shall He not with Him also freely give us all things." –Romans 8:32

"... For this purpose the Son of God was manifested, that He might destroy the works of the devil." –I John 3:8b

"Beloved, I wish above all things that thou mayest prosper, and be in good health, even as thy soul prospered." –III John 2

"Who his own self bore our sins in his own body on the tree, that we being dead to sins, should live unto righteousness: by whose stripes ye were healed." –I Peter 2:24

"He sent His word, and healed them, and delivered them from their destruction." –Psalm 107:20

"I will praise thee with my whole heart; before the gods will I sing praise unto thee. I will worship toward thy holy temple, and praise thy name for thy loving kindness and for thy truth, for thou hast magnified thy word above all thy name. In the day when I cried, thou answered me, and strengthened me with strength in my soul. All the kings of the earth shall praise thee. O Lord, when they hear the words of thy mouth. Yea, they shall sing in the ways of the Lord: for great is the glory of the Lord. Though the Lord be high, yet hath he respects unto the lowly: but the proud he knows afar off. Though I walk in the midst of trouble, thou will revive me: thou shalt stretch forth thine hand against the wrath of mine enemies, and thine right hand shall save me. The Lord will perfect that which concerneth me thy mercy, O Lord endureth forever: forsake not the works of thine own hands." –Psalm 138

"Heal me, O Lord, and I shall be healed ..." –Jeremiah 17:14

"Behold, I will bring it health and cure, and I will cure them, and will reveal unto them the abundance of peace and truth." –Jeremiah 33:6

"Confess your faults one to the other, and pray one for another, that ye may be healed. The effectual fervent prayer of a righteous man avails much." –James 5:16

"The Lord opened the eyes of the blind." –Psalm 146:8

"The blind receive their sight." –Matthew 11:5

"The Lord upholdeth all that fall, and raiseth up all those that be bowed down." –Psalm 145:14

"Then shalt thou walk in thy way safely, and thy foot shall not stumble." –Proverbs 3:23

"If you diligently heed the voice of the Lord your God and do what is right in His sight, give ear to His commandments and keep all His statutes, I will put none of these diseases on you which I have brought on the Egyptians. For I am the Lord who heals you." –Exodus 15:26

"Before Isaiah had left the middle court, the word of the Lord came to him. 'Go back and tell Hezekiah, the ruler of my people, This is what the Lord, the God of your father David, says: I have heard your prayer and seen your tears; I will heal you. On the third day from now you will go up to the temple of the Lord. I will add fifteen years to your life. And I will deliver you and this city from the hand of the king of Assyria. I will defend this city for my sake and for the sake of my servant David.'" –2 Kings 4-6

ACKNOWLEDGMENTS

I would like to offer my deepest gratitude:

To my husband, my children, and my parents, who in all of their own ways did the very best they could to help me while fending for themselves throughout this journey. To my two sisters for doing what only sisters can do. For years I prided myself as the glue in my family, making it difficult on everyone while I was ill.

To Dr. Rollin Thrift, who is a very rare human being. In over thirty-five years of knowing him, I've heard him upset twice, and never to the point of being unable to be sensible. He is intelligent, kind, compassionate, selfless, and a great husband to my sister. He has always made the time for our physical, mental, and spiritual well-being during countless encounters during this journey. He remains a constant source of professional medical advice. He continues to encourage our family through telephone and sit-down conversations. He does this in addition to working in the ER of several medical centers.

To Dr. Marsha Thigpen, who single-handedly trained me with the medical knowledge that enabled me to fight for myself. To Dr. Jim & Susan Byrum, Paula, and the entire Garret-Goss clinic for never leaving our side. To Dr. Richard Burt, Amey Morgan, Carol Burns, and the transplant teams of Northwestern Memorial Medical Center and Prentis Women's Hospital of Chicago for pre-transplant, transplant, and post-transplant care.

To our First Baptist Church family of Bentonville, Arkansas; Dave Roberts and Beth Sevey; our community in Northwest Arkansas; "the Calvary" in Little Rock; my new-found friends on this journey, including Genet (I wouldn't want your job; since we met you have been a source of hope when I just couldn't write another word); and the grand host of other loving, supporting family, friends, and professionals who allowed yourselves to do the work of the Lord during this process.

I know I have forgotten someone, because so many poured out their expressions of love for us. Please do not hold that against me, but forgive and love me instead. There is no way we could have made it without all of you.

Finally, to the neuromyelitis optica community: you are not alone. I am and will always be here for you as long as I am alive. I wake up and go to sleep thinking about whom I can serve, and how to help them win their NMO battle. This mission is my lifestyle. I do not have a big corporation, or a philanthropist supporting this necessary work, but I completely trust God to fulfill His promises. Be sure to reach out when you need to. Having NMO is not your fault. NMO does not define who you are.

RESOURCES

American Autoimmune & Related Diseases
22100 Gratiot Ave.
Eastpointe, MI 48021
Phone: (586) 776-3900
Toll-free: (800) 598-4668
Email: aarda@aarda.org
Website: www.aarda.org

AutoImmunity Community
Website: www.facebook.com/autoimmunityforum

Genetic and Rare Diseases (GARD) Information Center
PO Box 8126
Gaithersburg, MD 20898-8126
Phone: (301) 251-4925
Toll-free: (888) 205-2311
Website: rarediseases.info.nih.gov/GARD/

Guthy-Jackson Charitable Foundation
Allocates 100% of all donations directly to NMO research.
8910 University Center Lane, Suite 725
San Diego, CA 92122
Phone: (858) 638-7638
Email: info@guthyjacksonfoundation.org
Website: www.guthyjacksonfoundation.org

Living to Win Foundation
Bentonville, Arkansas
Website: www.livingtowin.org

National Organization for Rare Disorders (NORD)
55 Kenosia Avenue
Danbury, CT 06810
Phone: 203-744-0100
Website: rarediseases.org

NIH/National Institute of Neurological Disorders and Stroke
P.O. Box 5801
Bethesda, MD 20824
Phone: (301) 496-5751
Toll-free: (800) 352-9424
Website: www.ninds.nih.gov

Transverse Myelitis Association
1787 Sutter Parkway
Powell, OH 43065-8806 USA

Phone: (614) 766-1806
Email: info@myelitis.org
Website: www.myelitis.org

Trials

Information on current clinical trials is posted at www. clinicaltrials.gov. All studies receiving U.S. government funding, and some supported by private industry, are posted on this government website.

For information about clinical trials being conducted at the NIH Clinical Center in Bethesda, MD, contact the NIH Patient Recruitment Office:
Tollfree: (800) 411-1222
TTY: (866) 411-1010
Email: prpl@cc.nih.gov

For information about clinical trials sponsored by private sources, contact:
www.centerwatch.com

For information about clinical trials conducted in Europe, contact:
https://www.clinicaltrialsregister.eu/

CPSIA information can be obtained
at www.ICGtesting.com
Printed in the USA
JSHW031407220322
24109JS00001B/7